LOOKING BACK AT BRITAIN

THE END OF A WORLD

1910s

LOOKING BACK AT BRITAIN

THE END OF A WORLD

1910s

Jeremy Harwood

Reader's Digest | gettyimages®

CONTENTS

1910s IMAGE GALLERY
FRONT COVER: Men and women working alongside each other in a shell filling factory in about 1916
BACK COVER: A British 'Tommy', fully equipped and ready for the front, photographed by Henry Mayson in his studio in Keswick.
TITLE PAGE: A bus conductress collects fares on the top deck in winter. Women were employed on the buses for the first time during the First World War, but their jobs went back to men when the war was over.
OPPOSITE: A British soldier on a Rudge Multi motorcycle, with two of his colleagues behind, shortly before going out to France in 1914.
FOLLOWING PAGES:
Cyclists stand on their saddles for a peek over the fence at the Hendon Aviation meeting in 1911.
A Decca gramophone provides the entertainment for a peaceful boating day out in August 1919.
Women and children scavenging for coal on the local slag heap during the miners' strike of 1912.
A machine gun regiment of the Royal Northumberland Fusiliers, also known as 'The Fighting Fifth', in April 1916 after the Battle of St Eloi, south of Ypres. They are equipped with the Lewis Gun, a US-invented light machine gun powered by gas.

THE END OF
AN ERA

It was a tumultuous start to a momentous decade. Two bitter general elections were fought in the space of a year to decide whether peers or people governed the nation. The Conservatives fought relentlessly to stop the Liberal government granting Home Rule to Ireland, especially after the Parliament Act removed the power of the House of Lords to veto legislation passed by the Commons. Beyond Parliament, labour unrest was rife, with strikes breaking out on a record-breaking scale. Women were demanding the right to vote, with suffragettes prepared to go to prison for their cause. But then, in faraway Sarajevo, the Austrian Archduke Franz Ferdinand was assassinated. Within weeks, Britain was embroiled in the First World War.

ALL DRESSED UP The 16-year-old Prince Edward and his sister, Princess Mary, pose in their finery for the coronation of their father. For the young prince, the highlight of the ceremony was doffing his coronet and kneeling to pledge allegiance to the newly crowned George V.

PEERS VERSUS PEOPLE

It was nothing less than a battle over who ruled. The Liberals had secured an overwhelming majority in the House of Commons in the general election of 1906, but the Conservatives – or Unionists as they then preferred to be known – were masters of the House of Lords. Some 475 of the 602 peers were Unionists; less than 90 were Liberals. Arthur Balfour, the defeated Unionist leader, was quick to capitalise on the situation. It was everyone's duty, he thundered in Nottingham, just four days after losing his parliamentary seat in Manchester, to ensure that 'the great Unionist Party should still control, whether in power or whether in opposition, the destinies of this great Empire'. Egged on by Balfour, the Lords proceeded to slaughter many cherished Liberal measures, either by amending them out of all recognition or rejecting them outright.

The Education Bill was the peers' first victim, followed by the Plural Voting Bill. The Lords then forced the government to postpone its Licensing Bill; when this finally reached them, in November 1908, they showed little mercy. They did allow the Old Age Pensions Bill to go through that same month, even though many of them heartily disliked the measure, but the following year they fought tooth and nail against David Lloyd George's controversial budget. When the budget reached the House of Lords, in November 1909, Lord Lansdowne, leader of the Unionist peers, denounced it as 'a monument of reckless and improvident

YOUNG LIBERALS
Schoolboy supporters – all, bar the driver of the wagon, not yet old enough to vote – parade in support of Sir Stephen Collins, the Liberal candidate for the Lambeth Kennington constituency, in the first of the two General Elections held in 1910. Collins had first won election to the House of Commons in the Liberal landslide victory of 1906; he held his seat until 1918, when, like many of his fellow Liberals who supported Asquith, the party leader, he was defeated by a Coalition candidate in the election that followed the end of the First World War. Collins was one of many Liberal backbenchers who supported the administration in pressing to force Lloyd George's radical 1909 Budget through the Lords. There was growing determination among government MPs to curb the power of the House of Lords to veto legislation that the Commons wished to become law.

AWAY FROM IT ALL

Herbert Asquith, who succeeded Sir Henry Campbell-Bannerman as Prime Minister of the Liberal government in 1908, is pictured (seated second from right) taking a country break from the cares of office with some of his supporters. Asquith needed all his wits about him as the new decade dawned. Though the House of Lords eventually let David Lloyd George's budget through, Asquith faced a constitutional crisis. The Liberals were determined to strip the peers of their power of veto; the Opposition was determined to resist the move at all costs. Tempers boiled over in the House of Commons on 24 July, 1910, when Asquith was howled down by Unionist backbenchers as soon as he rose to speak. For 30 minutes, he tried in vain to make himself heard. 'It was', Winston Churchill, the Home Secretary, reported to the King, 'a squalid, frigid, organised attempt to insult the Prime Minister.'

finance'. It was rejected by an overwhelming 350 votes to 75. The government responded immediately by dissolving Parliament and calling a General Election.

The ensuing election of January 1910 was a bitter contest. Herbert Asquith, the Liberal Prime Minister, told his East Fife constituents that the Lords had 'violated the constitution' by rejecting the budget, in a 'proceeding without precedent'. The pugnacious Lloyd George had warned peers of the consequences if they rejected his budget – 'they are forcing a revolution and they will get it', he told a cheering audience in Limehouse. He claimed that the wishes of the vast majority of ordinary folk across the land were being thwarted by 'five hundred men, chosen accidentally from among the unemployed'. Winston Churchill, the Home Secretary, was as scathing as the Chancellor, calling for 'a smashing blow from the electors to finish it off forever'.

'… a played-out, obsolete, anachronistic assembly, a survival of a feudal arrangement utterly passed out of its original meaning, a force long since passed away …'

Winston Churchill, on the House of Lords

An unforeseen development

Despite the electoral rhetoric, the Liberals lost heavily and saw their great 1906 majority melt away. They still dominated in Scotland and Wales, but the Unionists, with a net gain of 116 seats, became the majority party in England. In the end the two were evenly balanced with the Liberals on 275 seats and the Unionists on 273, but the government could also count on the support of the 82 Irish Nationalists and a growing band of 40 Labour MPs. This gave Asquith a majority of 112.

Though the House of Lords was now grudgingly prepared to let the budget through, the Liberals were still determined to curb the legislative powers of the upper house. But the premier had a problem. Edward VII's private secretary, Lord Knollys, had warned Asquith that the King 'would not be justified in creating new peers until after a second General Election'. Without the new peers to override the Conservative majority – or a meaningful threat that they would be created – there was no chance of passing legislation of the kind the Liberals had in mind.

Asquith soldiered on. Carefully drafted resolutions, setting out the government's plan, were laid before the House of Commons in April 1910. The Parliament Bill was to follow and Conservative diehards readied themselves for all-out resistance. Not only did they detest the planned legislation, but they also knew that, if it became law, Home Rule for Ireland would almost certainly follow – a move they were determined to prevent at all costs. The country was on the brink of the greatest constitutional crisis it had faced for centuries. Then something happened that no one had foreseen. The King collapsed and died.

RADICAL PARTNERSHIP
Chancellor of the Exchequer David Lloyd George, his wife Margaret, Winston Churchill – newly promoted to Home Secretary – and William Clarke (right), the Chancellor's private secretary, march across Parliament Square. The Chancellor was on his way to introduce the 1910 budget. Lloyd George and Churchill were close friends and usually supported each other in debates in Cabinet. Newspaper proprietor Sir George Riddell wrote 'they act in the closest co-operation and are obviously impressed with each other's powers.' Some Liberals – including Margot Asquith, the Prime Minister's wife – did their best to break up the relationship. After the January 1910 election, she warned Churchill against copying the Chancellor in the violence of his language. 'Believe me', she wrote to the Home Secretary, 'cheap scores, hen-roost phrases & oratorical want of dignity is out of date.' For her part, Margaret Lloyd George disliked Churchill intensely. It made no difference. The two men remained firm political partners.

THE DEATH OF THE KING

Edward VII had been ailing for some time. That April, at the insistence of his doctors, he went to Biarritz for a much-needed holiday, but he returned looking almost as exhausted as before. He then suffered an acute attack of bronchitis, but despite being desperately ill, he insisted on continuing to work. Queen Alexandra was called back early from a Mediterranean cruise, but even she could not persuade Edward to take it easy.

When it came, the end was sudden. On 6 May, after toying with a light luncheon in his bedroom at Buckingham Palace, the King decided to play with his canaries, whose cage stood by the window curtains. As he tried to cross the room, he fell to the floor. It was clear that he was suffering a series of heart attacks, but he refused to be helped to bed. Instead, he sat in a chair, protesting: 'No, I shall not give in; I shall go on; I shall work to the end.'

After a brief examination, Edward's doctors agreed that there was no hope. They administered morphia for the pain and the Archbishop of Canterbury was summoned. While the Archbishop waited in an antechamber, the Prince of Wales told his father that one of his racehorses had won the 4.15 at Kempton Park. 'I am very glad', the King murmered in reply. They were the last coherent words he spoke. He lapsed into a coma, which allowed his nurses to undress him and put him to bed. Shortly before midnight, with the Archbishop and Alexandra at his bedside, Edward VII passed away peacefully. The Prince of Wales, now George V, wrote: 'I have lost my best friend and the best of fathers.'

CLOSE TO DEATH
Concerned members of the public crowd respectfully against the railings outside Buckingham Palace to read the latest medical bulletin detailing the King's condition. The news of Edward VII's sudden collapse stunned the capital. 'London tonight,' the *New York Times* reported, 'is a despairing city … Even the physiognomy of the streets showed a sudden change. Thoroughfares which are normally scenes of life, bustle and gaiety resemble the streets of a city through which the shadow of death has stalked.' Shortly before midnight on 6 May, 1910, it was all over. The much-loved King was dead and a grieving nation mourned.

In
Loving Memory
of

Edward VII. Peacemaker,
King AND Emperor.
MAY 6TH 1910.

ROYAL FUNERAL

On the day of the funeral, 20 May, the country came to a standstill. In Sussex, Rudyard Kipling recorded how, apart from the birds singing, there was not a sound to be heard. All rail traffic had been halted in honour of the dead King. The funeral procession was an imposing one. The new King George V rode behind the gun-carriage bearing his father's coffin, with his cousin Kaiser Wilhelm II of Germany beside him. Then followed the kings of Belgium, Bulgaria, Denmark, Greece, Norway, Portugal and Spain. Other royals present included Archduke Franz Ferdinand, heir to the Austro-Hungarian throne, and Marie Feodorovna, sister of Queen Alexandra and Dowager Empress of Russia. Former president Theodore Roosevelt represented the USA. Edward's favourite charger – riding boots reversed in the stirrups as a sign of respect – took part in the royal funeral procession, here seen arriving at Paddington Station. He is followed by little Caesar, the King's favourite fox terrier, walking disconsolately with a Highland servant, perhaps the most poignant sight of all. The King's coffin was loaded reverently onto a special train to Windsor, where his remains were buried in St George's Chapel. The memorial card (above) commemorates Edward's achievements as a peacemaker, king and emperor.

HEIR AND SUCCESSOR
A curious portrait of George V, taken around 1910 shortly before his succession, in the act of lighting a cigarette. A passion for the habit was one of the things that father and son had in common. George was more reserved than his fun-loving father, but perhaps that was appropriate to the changing times. Just three years after George rode with his cousin, Willhelm II of Germany, behind Edward's coffin, their two nations would be on the brink of war.

The nation was distraught. There was, said Lord Morley, the Secretary of State for India, a 'sense of personal loss in a way deeper and keener than when Queen Victoria died'. One of the dying King's last visitors, with the consent of his wife Alexandra, was Alice Keppel, the King's last mistress. Her husband Colonel Keppel told one of his daughters: 'Nothing will ever be quite the same again.' The Prime Minister received the news by wireless on board the Admiralty yacht *Enchantress* as it steamed homewards from Gibraltar through the Bay of Biscay. Asquith later recorded: 'I went up on deck, and I remember well that the first sight that met my eyes in the twilight before dawn was Halley's comet blazing in the sky … I felt bewildered and indeed stunned.'

It was a sentiment that millions shared. Edward's body lay in state in Westminster Hall from 17 to 19 May, and some 250,000 people filed silently past to pay their last respects. Hundreds of thousands lined the streets the next day to watch the procession pass. Many thousands more lined the tracks to Windsor as the funeral train puffed slowly by.

A CONSTITUTIONAL CRISIS

Once Edward's funeral was over, life began to return to normal. Many expected the Royal Ascot race-meeting to be cancelled, but George V declared it should go ahead – given Edward's love of racing, this seemed fitting. Gazing down from the stands above the racecourse, Elizabeth, Countess of Fingall, noticed the large black feathered hats worn by every woman in the crowd. It made it look, she though, as if 'an enormous flight of crows had just settled'.

The social season may have resumed, but Parliament had reached an impasse. Asquith was reluctant to press an inexperienced ruler, at the very start of his reign, to create the new peers needed to force the Parliament Act through the House of Lords. Instead, supported by his Cabinet colleagues, Asquith said he was prepared to explore the possibility of a compromise. Even parts of the Tory press supported his point of view. James Garvin, the influential editor of *The Observer*, led the way by calling for a political truce and an inter-party conference. It was the duty of the Unionist leaders, Garvin stated, to spare the new sovereign from becoming embroiled in the 'fiercest of partisan fights'. The Unionists agreed to take part.

The so-called Constitutional Conference began on 17 June, 1910, and met 12 times before suspending activities for the summer holidays. It reconvened for further talks in October and November, but still failed to reach agreement. Predictably, the sticking point was Home Rule. The Liberals – represented by Asquith, Lloyd George, Lord Crewe (leader of the House of Lords) and Augustine Birrell (Chief Secretary for Ireland) – refused to accede to the Unionist demand that any Home Rule Bill be exempt from the operation of the Parliament Act. Instead, they proposed that if such a bill were rejected twice by the Lords, it should be put to the people in a national referendum. The Unionists, for their part, rejected Lloyd George's call for the formation of a coalition government with an agreed programme on all the main issues of the day.

Asquith had no choice but to call another election and ask the King for a promise to create new peers. Like his father, George was unwilling to agree, but in the end he gave way. 'After a long talk,' he recorded in his diary, 'I agreed most reluctantly to give the Cabinet a secret understanding that, in the event of the Government being returned with a majority … I should use my Prerogative to make peers if asked for.' With this pledge in his pocket, Asquith went to the country in December confident of victory, but the result was almost a re-run of the previous election. The voters were bored with the endless constitutional struggle. They wanted it resolved with no more appeals to the country.

The siege of Sidney Street

What was really gripping public attention in the bitter cold January of 1911 was an armed clash in a street in Houndsditch in London, which led to the army being ordered into action. A band of exiled Russian and Latvian anarchists had taken refuge among the foreign community in London's East End. Previously, in 1909, they had been involved in an incident in Tottenham, when two anarchists had shot and killed a policeman while trying to steal the weekly wages being delivered to a local rubber factory. One of the anarchists killed himself and 27 bystanders were

UNDER FIRE
In December 1910, three City of London policemen were killed and two seriously injured while trying to arrest a gang of foreign anarchists detected trying to tunnel into an East End jeweller's shop. In the massive manhunt that followed, three of the gang were tracked down to a lodging house in Sidney Street. Winston Churchill, the ebullient Home Secretary, was quick to take personal charge of the situation.

On 3 January, 1911, 300 policemen surrounded the house, supported by soldiers of the Scots Guards who had been rushed to the scene by Churchill. During the shoot-out that followed, the building caught fire, but the anarchists still refused to surrender; they shot at the Fire Brigade when firemen tried to intervene. Two of the anarchists died in the siege, but the corpse of their leader, the notorious 'Peter the Painter', was never found.

injured. 'Who are these fiends in human shape?' the *Daily Mirror* cried, then went on to answer its own question. 'The answer is they are foreign anarchists, men who have been expelled from Russia for their crimes; whose political creed and religion is that human life is of no value at all.'

Special Branch believed that Christian Jalmish, a young Latvian otherwise known as Jacob Fogel, was the leader of the gang in the 'Tottenham Outrages' as they were christened by the press. His followers included Peter Piatkow, swiftly dubbed 'Peter the Painter', who in December 1910 was caught with some other Latvians in the act of tunnelling into a jeweller's shop in Houndsditch. They promptly opened fire, killing three police officers, before retreating back up the tunnel. Almost three weeks later, they were tracked to a house in Sidney Street, where they barricaded themselves in.

The police sent an urgent request for reinforcements to Winston Churchill, the Home Secretary. A detachment of Scots Guards were immediately sent to the scene, and a battery of horse artillery was also ordered up, though in the event this did not go into action. Churchill hurried to Sidney Street to take personal charge of the siege operations. The anarchists chose to perish, rather than surrender. Seeing that their position was untenable, they set fire to the house. When the police and troops finally managed to break in, they found two charred bodies in the ruins. One had been shot; the other had been asphyxiated.

THE CORONATION SUMMER

There was one event in particular that people looked forward to that summer of 1911: the coronation of George V and Queen Mary. It went ahead on schedule on 22 June. As the King noted that morning, the weather was 'overcast and cloudy', but that did not deter spectators cramming into the crimson stands that lined the processional route from Buckingham Palace to Westminster Abbey.

The Abbey slowly filled up with notables invited to attend the ceremony. Among them were Rudyard Kipling and his wife, who had made an early start from their Sussex home to drive up to London by motor car. Kipling spotted Richard Haldane, the Secretary of State for War, scurrying up the aisle with his peer's robes askew, resembling, Kipling thought, 'a Toby dog strayed from a Punch and Judy Show'. Queen Mary arrived looking 'pale and strained', according to the Master of Elibank, the Liberal Chief Whip. Finally, the King entered the Abbey.

The climax of the long service came when the Archbishop of Canterbury placed the crown on the King's head. The young Prince of Wales then approached the throne, doffed his coronet and on bended knee pledged allegiance, before rising to kiss his father on both cheeks. Queen Mary's crowning followed. It was an occasion, and a spectacle, that no one who witnessed it would ever forget.

After the King and Queen had departed, the Abbey slowly emptied and the cleaners moved in to sweep up. They found three ropes of pearls, 20 brooches,

WINDOW WATCHERS
Female factory workers watch George V's coronation procession pass by on the street below. The day started off grey and clammy, but this did not deter the thousands who packed the processional route. The Abbey filled up quickly with guests. Some, like Lady Huntingdon, had set off as early as six o'clock that morning to make sure of being in their seats in good time. Some 6,000

stools and chairs, carved of fine mahogany and emblazoned with a coronet, were made especially for the ceremony. Each one had the name of its intended occupant painstakingly inscribed on its back. Being invited to attend the ceremony did not necessarily guarantee a good view. Lady Ottoline Morrell found herself perched so high at the top of the Abbey that she could hardly see anything at all.

'To his great father's throne!
Make doubly welcome Alexandra's
son – Thy son, O England!'

Florence Earl Coates, Coronation Ode, 1911

CROWNING A NEW KING AND QUEEN

George V and Queen Mary pose for their official photograph in full coronation regalia (left). The picture was taken shortly before they drove in procession from Buckingham Palace to Westminster Abbey for the actual coronation ceremony. Both approached the occasion with some degree of trepidation. The King worried about the weather; the Queen feared that the swaying of the unsprung royal carriage that was to take her and her husband to the Abbey might trigger off her propensity to sea-sickness. She also worried that the King's knock knees might mar the dignity of his procession up the aisle. But all went well, and in the end the event was considered a triumph. Afterwards, the attending Lord and Ladies could relax (above), while the public flocked to buy souvenir postcards commemorating the great occasion (right). The Duke of Devonshire was mightily relieved that everything had gone so smoothly. Two weeks earlier, after attending a somewhat chaotic coronation rehearsal, he had noted in his diary: 'Nobody knew what to do. Good deal of confusion.'

'... the ceremony ... was an awful ordeal for us both.'

Queen Mary, in a letter to her Aunt Augusta

HEAT WAVE
Children enjoy a paddle in a man-made seaside playground in Fulham, southwest London, in July 1910. If that summer was hot, the following one – the Coronation summer – was even hotter. After a cold April, the temperature rose inexorably until, by the end of July, the heat was unbearable. Those who could afford it headed for the coast. The Churchills – Winston had married Clementine Hozier, grand-daughter of the 10th Earl of Airlie, in September 1908 – took a house in fashionable Broadstairs in Kent. Fellow-visitor Neville Lytton described Clementine as coming forth 'like the reincarnation of Venus re-entering the sea'.

half a dozen bracelets, 20 golden balls that had fallen off coronets and three-quarters of a diamond necklace. All jewels were safely returned to their owners. Queen Mary was greatly relieved that it had all gone so well. Writing to her Aunt Augusta in Germany she commented: 'You may imagine what an immense relief it is to us that the great and solemn ceremony of Thursday is now over …'

The Coronation day had been peaceful – the police reported not one arrest. After it, the festivities continued. The Wimbledon tennis championships began on 26 June, and true to form the weather on the opening day was unsettled. The *Daily Telegraph* noted 'the familiar spectacle of sodden courts and idling players'. That evening, the King and Queen attended a gala ballet performance given in their honour by Russian impresario Sergei Diaghilev's Ballets Russes. The Russian dancers were the artistic sensation of the season. Leonard Woolf, then a young civil servant just back from Ceylon, wrote that he had 'never seen anything more perfect, nor more exciting on any stage'. The actress Ellen Terry declared that, thanks to the Russians, the art of dance had been restored to its 'primal nobility'.

Investing a new Prince of Wales

On 7 July, George V and Queen Mary left the capital for a coronation tour of Wales, Ireland and Scotland. Their first task was to preside over the investiture of Edward, their eldest son, as Prince of Wales. A 10,000-strong crowd witnessed the event, which took place in the ruins of Caernarfon Castle, transformed, so one onlooker recorded, into 'a medieval tilting gallery' for the occasion.

Next to the Royal Family, Lloyd George, himself a proud Welshman, was the star of the show. He had coached the 17-year-old Prince in Welsh, so that Edward could address the people of the Principality in their own language. Prince and politician were greeted with tremendous cheers. For Lloyd George, this was a far cry from Coronation Day, when he had been booed by some in the stands reserved for MPs. Winston Churchill, as Home Secretary, also had a task to perform. He proclaimed the long list of titles with which the Prince had just been invested, and he managed the task without a single slip. Later, he told the Prince that he had practised reciting the list on the golf course for hours.

Crisis in the Lords

Back in London, where the weather had turned scorching, there was more trouble ahead as the political temperature rose even further. The Parliament Bill had been returned to the Commons, but the amendments the Lords had made to it rendered it toothless. The government now asked the King to allow them to make public his promise to create peers. The King agreed. Accordingly, Asquith wrote to Balfour and Lord Lansdowne, telling them that 'should the necessity arise, the Government will advise the King to exercise his Prerogative to secure the passing into Law of the Bill in substantially the same form in which it left the House of Commons.'

The sting was in the tail. 'His Majesty', Asquith concluded, 'has been pleased to signify that he will consider it his duty to accept, and act, on that advice.'

By this time, the Unionist peers had split into two factions. There were the diehards, the so-called 'Ditchers', led by Lord Halsbury, who were ready to defy the House of Commons regardless of the consequences, and the 'Hedgers' who were prepared to vote with the government or at least abstain. The vote took place late in the evening of 10 August. By 131 votes (81 Liberals, 13 Bishops and 37 Unionists) to 114 diehards, the Lords resolved not to insist on their amendments to the Parliament Act; it was law at last. The King wrote in his diary: 'So the Halsburyites, thank God, were beaten and I am spared any further humiliation.'

Trouble from abroad – show-down at Agadir

Sir Edward Grey, the Foreign Secretary, had other things on his mind. A major international crisis was brewing following the arrival of the *Panther*, a German gunboat, off the port of Agadir in Morocco. The French regarded North Africa as their own particular sphere of influence, but Germany now demanded territorial concessions. The big question was which side would Britain support?

Thanks largely to the diplomacy of Edward VII, Britain's relations with France had vastly improved in recent years, with the cultivation of what was christened an *entente cordiale* between the two nations. Meanwhile relations with Germany, despite close royal connections, had deteriorated. Most Britons had a hearty dislike of Kaiser Wilhelm II, whose determination to create a High Seas Fleet big enough to challenge the Royal Navy's supremacy at sea had resulted in a hugely expensive naval race, with both countries building more and bigger warships.

ANTI-SEMITISM IN BRITAIN
A Jewish couple stand in the doorway of their shop in South Wales, which was vandalised in anti-Semitic riots in the summer of 1911. What caused the riots remains unclear. They lasted a week and Winston Churchill, then Home Secretary, sent in troops from the Worcester Regiment to suppress what he tersely labelled 'a pogrom'. The rioting started at Tredegar, where many had suffered as a result of the previous year's coal strike. According to one observer, some '200 young fellows' took to the streets to attack Jewish shops while 'singing several favourite Welsh hymn tunes'. The trouble spread to the neighbouring Gwent valley towns of Ebbw Vale, Rhymney, Cwm, Abertysswg, Brymawr and Senghennydd, where two Jewish-owned stores were burned to the ground. Many speculated about what had caused the rioting. Some said it was because the shops had put prices up, others that Jewish landlords had increased rents. The *Jewish World* condemned the rioters as criminals, but *The Times* reported that the attackers were 'respectable people to all appearances.'

The tensions found their way into the novels and drama of the day. William Le Queux had a bestseller with a gripping thriller called *The Great Invasion* of 1910. The plot revolved around a full-scale German landing in Britain. The novel's success was due in part to the *Daily Mail*, which advertised its serialisation of the book by hiring a troupe of out-of-work actors to goose-step though the West End dressed in Prussian uniform. On stage, Guy du Maurier's *An Englishman's Home* played to packed houses with its depiction of an unsuccessful attempt at invasion by thinly disguised 'Norlanders' in the service of the 'Empress of the North'. The patriotic fervour displayed by du Maurier's audience inspired the War Office to set up a recruiting booth for the new Territorial Army in the theatre's foyer; some 20,000 volunteers came forward in the first seven weeks of the production.

No one was prepared to put up with any more bombast from the Kaiser. It was the Chancellor, Lloyd George – up until then considered by many to be a pacifist, given what his outspoken stance had been in the Boer War – who made Britain's position crystal clear. Addressing diners at a banquet in the Mansion House, he warned: 'If a situation were to be forced on us in which peace could only be preserved ... by allowing Britain to be treated where her interests were vitally affected as if she was of no consequence in the Cabinet of nations, then I say emphatically that peace at that price would be a humiliation intolerable for a great country like ours to endure.' In the event, Germany and France came to terms over Morocco. War was averted – for now.

'WAKE UP ENGLAND'
A scene from *An Englishman's Home*, a hit play by Guy du Maurier, which opened to critical and public acclaim in London's West End in January 1909 and was still playing to packed houses well over a year later. Du Maurier, an uncle of the famous novelist Daphne du Maurier, was a serving officer in the Royal Fusiliers concerned by the apparent unpreparedness of the country to deal with a determined foreign invasion. His theme echoed the fears of many notables of the day, including Lord Roberts – the former commander-in-chief of the army who, in retirement, became the president of the National Service League – who was calling for the urgent introduction of peacetime conscription.

INDUSTRIAL AND SOCIAL STRIFE

The North African crisis was not the only emergency faced by the government. The Cabinet had to address a major dock strike and a still more threatening railway dispute. Both were part of an industrial upheaval that contemporaries called the 'Great Labour Unrest'. The unrest had started in autumn 1910, when miners in South Wales went on strike after local colliery owners locked out the union members at some of the pits. That November riots broke out in Tonypandy and the Home Secretary, Winston Churchill, ordered in police reinforcements and troops – the latter kept in reserve. By the time calm was restored, one striker had been killed and more than 500 injured.

continued on page 36

STRIKES AND LOCKOUTS

Contemporaries called it the 'Great Labour Unrest'. In 1909, some 2,690,000 working days were lost in strikes. Year on year that number rose relentlessly: to 9,870,000 in 1910; 10,160,000 in 1911; then, in 1912, a staggering 40,890,000 working days lost. The actual number of strikes was relatively small, but they were in vital industries – such as the pits, railways and docks – and on a national scale. It was little wonder that some feared revolution might be just around the corner.

STRIKERS AND SCABS
Members of the National Union of Clerks, wearing masks to conceal their faces, march to Hyde Park (below) to demand better pay and conditions. They were not alone in their protests. Footballers went on strike, albeit briefly, and strike action threw the music halls into confusion. Some employers responded by locking strikers out and bringing in blackleg labourers – the strikers called them scabs. The stokers (right) were among workers recruited by colliery owners to try to keep one of the South Wales pits at Tonypandy running; in an attempt to drive down wages, the owners had locked the miners out in autumn 1910. Rioting broke out as the strikers tried to shut the colliery down. On 7 November, hundreds of striking miners marched on the pit. Trouble flared that evening when the strikers threw stones at policemen guarding the power station. The rioting swiftly spread to the town square, where it resumed the following day. By the time it ended, 500 miners – one of whom later died – and 80 policemen had been injured. Home Secretary Winston Churchill ordered troops and police reinforcements to the scene to keep order. Tonypandy and its surrounding villages resembled a military camp.

WOMEN AND CHILDREN

Women mineworkers pose on a pile of coal during the 1912 national coal strike. This picture was taken in Wigan, Lancashire. Not all strike scenes were as peaceful. Down in South Wales, women had joined with their striking husbands in fighting police and soldiers when renewed rioting broke out in Tonypandy on 22 November, 1910. A sympathetic local newspaper reported how they 'joined with the men in the unequal combat and displayed a total disregard of personal danger which was as admirable as it was foolhardy'. They were swiftly dubbed 'the Amazons of the coalfield'. As the strikes went on, times became harder and harder for the strikers. Women and children were forced to resort to scavenging coal from the slag heaps near the closed mines to try to keep their homes warm. There was suffering in London's East End, too, when, in July 1911, the dockers went on all-out strike. These children (below) are waiting for charity food hand-outs. Lord Davenport, chairman of the London Port Authority and leader of the employers' side, declared publicly that he would starve the dockers back to work. He succeeded. After staying out for a fortnight, the men were forced back to work on Davenport's terms.

'We will not allow the ordinary civil operations of strikers, of men on strike, to be hampered and interfered with by a needless display of force.'

J. Ramsay MacDonald, Labour leader, House of Commons, 1911

Things did not get any better the following year. Seamen went on strike at the time of the Coronation, followed by dockers in London, Liverpool, Hull, Bristol and Southampton. Riots in Liverpool led to 2,500 troops being dispatched to the city; a cruiser, anchored off Birkenhead, had its guns trained on the shore. At 30 hours' notice, four railway unions declared they were ready to call their members out. Despite a last-minute plea by the Prime Minister, the strike went ahead, paralysing the North and Midlands and partially affecting the south of the country.

Lloyd George was given the task of persuading the railwaymen back to work. In just 48 hours he succeeded and Asquith was quick to congratulate him: 'It is the latest, but by no means the least, of the loyal and invaluable services which you have rendered.' Yet the unrest continued. In January 1912 the Miner's Federation threatened a national strike to force a guaranteed minimum wage. When the mine-owners refused point-blank, the men came out. Eventually, the government was forced to impose compulsory wage machinery on the industry, but true to its laissez-faire beliefs, it refused to lay down what the new minimum rates should be. The London dockers struck again, but this time the employers held out for victory; the strike collapsed in July as impoverished dockers began to drift back to work.

Railwaymen, miners and dockers were by no means the only people to resort to strike action. Middle-class doctors threatened to strike in protest against rules imposed on them by Lloyd George's reforming National Insurance Act. In 1911 even schoolchildren came out on strike in 62 towns and villages up and down the country demanding longer lunch breaks and an end to corporal punishment.

Votes for women

Women were on the march with a simple demand: to be granted the right to vote. The suffragettes were divided into two camps: those who favoured peaceful persuasion and the militants, who were ready to take direct action. Not surprisingly, it was the latter – led by Mrs Emmeline Pankhurst and her daughter Christabel – who grabbed the headlines. Members of the Women's Social and Political Union (WSPU), urged on by their leaders, heckled politicians at public meetings, demonstrated outside Parliament, smashed shop windows and chained themselves to railings. Many were prepared to go to prison for their cause. Once there, they went on hunger strike and the Home Office responded by authorising the women to be forcibly fed.

Parliament – like the general public as a whole – was divided as to whether women should be granted the vote at all. Most Liberals were broadly in favour, but Prime Minister Asquith was totally opposed. Arthur Balfour and his successor as Unionist leader, Andrew Bonar Law, were prepared to see women get the vote, but most Unionist-Conservative MPs were emphatically against it. F E Smith, Tory politican and later Lord Chancellor, spoke for them – and for some Liberals, too – when he told the Commons of his 'implacable resistance' to any such measure. The activities of the militants probably led many of their initial supporters among MPs – notably Lloyd George and Churchill – to modify their views.

The government allowed a free vote on two women's suffrage bills introduced by backbenchers, but it refused to give up parliamentary time to ensure that either became law. There was a certain amount of political expedience behind this reluctance. To win Unionist support and to give the impression of moderation, the bills proposed that only a limited number of women – property owners aged over 30 – be granted the vote. Liberal leaders quickly saw that such legislation

MILITANT LEADER
Mrs Emmeline Pankhurst, founder of the Women's Social and Political Union, is unceremoniously arrested at a suffragette demonstration outside Buckingham Palace in early 1914 (right). Like many of her fellow suffragettes – including her daughters Sylvia and Christabel – Mrs Pankhurst was prepared to face prison, hunger strike and force-feeding for the sake of the cause. The fashionable young lady in the poster (bottom right) looks mild-mannered, but appearances could be deceptive and many otherwise law-abiding women were willing to go to extremes. Demonstrations saw windows being smashed, buildings set on fire, leading politicians heckled and even physically assaulted. The Prime Minister himself was not immune. While playing a round of golf with his daughter Violet, Asquith was ambushed by a group of suffragette militants who tried – unsuccessfully – to tear off his clothes. Increasingly, there seemed to be no lengths to which the militants were not prepared to go.

'You can find in every country, over and over again, occasions when the men of the country have despaired and some heroic woman has roused them.'

Lord Robert Cecil, House of Commons, May 1913, speaking on behalf of the Suffragette cause

would add a substantial number of Unionist voters to the electoral roll. Put to the vote in May 1912, the second Bill failed to get a second reading. Asquith now offered a significant compromise. The Reform Bill that the government was about to introduce would be amended to put women on the same voting basis as men. The amendment was due to be debated in January 1913, but just before it came up for debate the Speaker of the House ruled the proposal constitutionally unacceptable. Such an amendment, he declared, was so fundamental that the Bill

DYING FOR THE CAUSE

In June 1913 Emily Wilding Davison threw herself in front of the King's horse Anmer during the Epsom Derby. Horse and jockey escaped unscathed, but four days later Davison died of the head injuries she had sustained. She received a martyr's funeral. Her coffin (right), adorned with a simple wreath and the banner of the Women's Social and Political Union, was escorted by a suffragette guard of honour from London's Victoria to King's Cross Station then on to Morpeth, her home in Northumberland, where she was buried. The suffragette motto 'Deeds not Words' was carved on her tombstone. Emily Davison had joined the movement in 1906 and had already been jailed several times before her fatal action at the 1913 Epsom Derby. Some said that her dramatic gesture was a publicity stunt gone horribly wrong, but Mrs Pankhurst had no doubts that her colleague had deliberately sacrificed her life for the cause. 'Emily Davison,' she wrote, 'clung to her conviction that one great tragedy, the deliberate throwing into the breach of a human life, would put an end to the intolerable torture of women.'

itself would have to be withdrawn and reintroduced. To the suffragettes' fury, the government dropped the measure, offering instead to allow time for another private member's Bill, but when the time came it, too, was rejected.

Many felt that the militant suffragettes had not helped the cause, turning MPs against the campaign. In February 1913 groups of suffragettes smashed up the orchid house at Kew, set fire to post boxes and railway carriages, and even attempted to plant a bomb to destroy Lloyd George's newly built country retreat. Then, that June, Emily Wilding Davison became a martyr for the cause when she threw herself in front of the King's horse in the Derby. It was all to no avail. In February 1914, Lloyd George bluntly told a women's deputation that the position was 'quite hopeless as far as this Parliament is concerned'. Adding insult to injury, he blamed the suffragettes themselves, declaring that 'militant members have made it almost impossible for those Liberal leaders who are in favour of women's suffrage to address meetings in support of it'.

MURDER AND DISASTER

There was plenty of other news to keep newspaper readers occupied. In October 1910, Dr Hawley Harvey Crippen – the first criminal in history to be arrested with the aid of radio transmission – went on trial at the Old Bailey for the murder of his wife. He was caught after a dramatic chase that took pursuing Scotland Yard detective, Chief Inspector Walter Dew, across the Atlantic to Canada. Back in Britain, the jury took just 27 minutes to find Crippen guilty. He was executed at Pentonville prison on 23 November that year. Ethel le Neve, his mistress who had fled with him disguised as a boy, was acquitted of being an accessory to the crime.

Tragedy in the Antarctic

Just over a year later, events unfolded in the remotest part of the globe that proved even more gripping. In January 1912, Captain Robert Falcon Scott and four fellow explorers were in a race against time in the Antarctic wilderness. The venture had begun as an attempt to become the first men to reach the South Pole, but a Norwegian expedition, led by Roald Amundsen, beat them to it. For Scott and his companions, the journey became a desperate and heroic battle for survival. Petty Officer Edgar Evans was the first to die, followed by Captain Titus Oates. Crippled by frostbite and conscious that he was holding the party back, Oates calmly left the tent where he and his companions were sheltering and went out

TRANSATLANTIC PURSUIT
Face swathed in a scarf, Dr Hawley Harvey Crippen (below left) is escorted down the gangplank by Chief Inspector Dew. Crippen was accused of murdering his wife, Cora, who was also known by her stage name of Belle Elmore. The remains of a poisoned, dismembered body had been found in the cellar of the couple's London home at 39 Hilldrop Crescent. Though the sex of the body was not certain, it was assumed to be Cora, who had disappeared, and a manhunt for Crippen was launched. Meanwhile, in Antwerp, he boarded the SS *Montrose* bound for Canada with his mistress Ethel le Neve (below), posing as a merchant and his 16-year-old son. The captain was suspicious and radioed to the ship's owners that he thought he had 'Crippen London cellar murderer and accomplice' on board. Dew promptly followed on a faster ship, reaching the St Lawrence River before them, where he boarded the *Montrose* and made his arrests before they could disembark.

STRUGGLING SOUTH
As the *Terra Nova* carried Captain Robert Scott and his expedition to the Antarctic (right), he confidently expected to become the first man to reach the South Pole. Here, the ship forces her way through the pack ice: it took three weeks to regain open water. It was hardly an auspicious start to Scott's quest. The expedition was short of funds and Scott was alarmed by the news that Roald Amundsen, the celebrated Norwegian explorer, had set off to try to get to the Pole before him.

into the teeth of a howling, freezing blizzard. His famous last words to his friends were: 'I am just going outside and may be some time.' Scott and the others knew that his sacrifice was to give them a better chance of survival.

The end came on 29 March, 1912, just 11 miles from their supply depot. Scott and his two remaining companions, Lieutenant Henry Bowes and Dr Edward Wilson, were trapped in their tent by yet another blizzard. With fuel and food exhausted, they rapidly grew weaker. In his final diary entry, Scott wrote: 'It seems a pity, but I do not think I can write more. For God's sake, look after our people.'

Sinking the unsinkable

The bodies of the three explorers were found by a search party in November, but before that, another disaster hit the headlines. On 15 April, 1912, the White Star liner RMS *Titanic* struck an iceberg as she steamed across the Atlantic on her maiden voyage. The ship sank beneath the waves within hours, taking two-thirds of those on board to their deaths: the ship did not carry enough lifeboats to accommodate all the passengers and crew.

The news devastated Britain. With its sister-ship *Olympic*, the *Titanic* was the biggest ocean liner ever built. No less an authority than *The Shipbuilder* had pronounced her 'practically unsinkable'. Rich and poor alike perished. Benjamin Guggenheim, the American multi-millionaire, refused even to contemplate pushing his way into a lifeboat. Instead, he and his valet retired below decks to change into evening dress. He told a steward: 'If we have to die, we will die like gentlemen.'

BIRTHDAY CELEBRATION
Captain Scott celebrating his birthday on 6 June, 1911, with members of his expedition. By November – the start of the brief Antarctic 'summer' – he was ready to set off for the South Pole with a hand-picked team of four companions. Unlike Amundsen, his Norwegian rival, who was equipped with sleds pulled by huskies, Scott's expedition was forced to rely on human muscle power: the newfangled motorised sledges they had taken with them proved a disaster, while the back-up Siberian ponies were unequal to the freezing conditions. The weather, too, turned against them. 'Our luck in weather is preposterous', Scott wrote in his diary. 'The conditions are simply horrible.' Nevertheless, he and his companions struggled on doggedly. On 16 January, 1912, they came across the remains of Amundsen's camp with a Norwegian flag tied to part of an abandoned sledge. 'This told us the whole story', Scott wrote. 'The Norwegians … are first at the Pole.' Scott and his four companions all perished as they attempted the return journey.

THE UNSINKABLE TITANIC

The White Star liner RMS *Titanic* steams slowly out of Queenstown harbour, Ireland, on her maiden voyage to New York in April 1912. The ship was a gigantic floating palace, the most luxurious liner in the world, and many rich passengers were on board just to be a part of her historic voyage. Many of them never reached their destination. On the night of 14 April, the *Titanic* was steaming at high speed when she struck an iceberg. If she had hit the iceberg head on, some believe, she may have survived, but she attempted to manoeuvre out of the way and the iceberg gouged a 90m slash along her starboard side. The ship sank within a matter of hours. More than 1,500 passengers and crew drowned; only 706 people managed to survive. Thomas Andrews, the naval architect who had designed the vessel, and Captain Edward Smith, in command for the ill-fated voyage, were among those who lost their lives. True to the tradition of the sea, Captain Smith made no effort to save himself, going down gallantly with his ship. When news of the disaster broke (left), many refused to believe it. Philip A S Franklin, vice-president of the White Star line in New York, said : 'I thought her unsinkable and I based my opinion on the best expert advice. I do not understand it.'

THE IRISH IMBROGLIO

As 1914 dawned, the government was facing yet another crisis. With the Parliament Act now in operation limiting the power of the Lords, the Liberals had kept their promise to the Irish Nationalists and introduced a third Home Rule Bill. Though the House of Lords still had the power to reject it twice, on its third submission the Bill would automatically become law.

But Ulster Loyalists were in no mood to accept any sort of Home Rule. They pledged that, should the Bill become law, they would set up a provisional government of their own to take over the province. Hundreds of thousands of Ulstermen – 471,444, it was claimed – signed a Solemn League and Covenant, binding themselves to fight Home Rule to their last breath. Back across the Irish Sea, Bonar Law and the other Unionist leaders encouraged the Ulster Loyalists in their defiance. At a rally of some 15,000 Unionist stalwarts at Blenheim, Bonar Law told the cheering audience that he could 'imagine no length of resistance to which Ulster can go in which I should not be prepared to support them, and which, in my belief, they would not be supported by the overwhelming majority of the British people.'

In response to pleas from King George, the two party leaders met secretly to seek a compromise. Asquith proposed that Ulster be given the chance to opt out of Home Rule for a number of years. Bonar Law demanded indefinite exclusion. Neither could agree on how much of the province should be excluded.

Mounting tension

The situation got worse when a decision to send troop reinforcements to Ulster provoked a mutiny. Brigadier-General Hubert Gough and 60 officers of the 3rd Cavalry Brigade, stationed at the Curragh outside Dublin, announced that they would resign their commissions rather than take part in any military operation in Ulster. They demanded that the government give a promise in writing that the army would not be used to quell opposition to Home Rule. John Seely, the incautious Secretary of State for War, duly gave them the assurance they sought. Asquith reacted immediately. Seely, together with General Sir John French and Sir John Ewart, the adjutant general, who had both agreed with the unfortunate letter, were all forced to resign. The Prime Minister then took control of the War Office himself.

Then, on 26 July, 1914, British troops opened fire on a stone-throwing crowd near Dublin. Three Irish Nationalists were killed and 38 wounded. That same month, George V convened a last-ditch conference at Buckingham Palace. The Speaker of the Commons took the chair, with Nationalist and Loyalist representatives from north and south participating, as well as the Liberal and Unionist leaders. The key issue, it transpired, was the future of two northern counties, Fermanagh and Tyrone. But neither side would give them up and as a result the conference collapsed in failure.

'ULSTER WILL FIGHT'
Sir Edward Carson, leader of the Ulster loyalists and one of the founders of the paramilitary Ulster Volunteers, signs the Solemn Oath of the Covenant in Belfast's City Hall in September 1912. He and his followers were pledged to resist the imposition of Home Rule on Ulster regardless of cost. By the following January, 100,000 Ulstermen aged between 17 and 65 had come forward, ready to take up arms if need be to defend the province and the Unionist cause – and the numbers kept on growing. There could be no compromise. When the Liberals offered Ulster the chance of opting out of Home Rule for six years, Carson threw the concession back in their faces. He told the House of Commons: 'We do not want sentence of death with a stay of execution for six years.' By August 1914, Ireland stood on the edge of potential civil war.

War in Europe looms

What might have happened next is a matter of conjecture, for other events intervened. The government intended to press on, but the Unionist leader Bonar Law persuaded Asquith to postpone legislation, arguing that 'to advertise our domestic dissensions at this time would weaken our influence for peace'.

On 28 June, 1914, while on a visit to Sarajevo in Bosnia-Herzegovina, Archduke Franz Ferdinand, the heir to the Austro-Hungarian throne, and his wife Sophie had been assassinated by a Bosnian-Serb nationalist. The Austrians, suspecting the hand of Serbia behind the murder, despatched an ultimatum to Serbia and began to mobilise their forces. Russia, France and Germany followed suit, lining up on different sides according to alliances. A European war was looking inevitable. The big question was what would Britain do? If negotiations to resolve the crisis failed, would she remain neutral or would she come to the support of France and Russia?

ALL OVER BY
CHRISTMAS

When Britain went to war with Germany on 4 August, 1914, no one anticipated that four years of devastating conflict were to follow. 'It will all be over by Christmas', was the popular refrain. David Lloyd George, who was Chancellor of the Exchequer at the start of the war, declared that it would be 'business as usual'. The Treasury's official view was that the war would have to end in 1915 as by then all the combatants would have run out of money. One man begged to differ. Lord Kitchener, the newly appointed Secretary of State for War, told disbelieving colleagues that the war would last for at least three years and that to fight it Britain would need to raise a mass army for the first time in its history. He called for a million volunteers to swell the ranks of the regular army.

FOND FAREWELL A British Tommy says goodbye to his family before joining his unit to embark for France. Mobilisation followed meticulous plans that had been laid out in the so-called War Book, compiled to provide a blueprint for action.

THE WAR BEGINS

As Europe lurched inexorably towards war, the British position was still far from clear. As late as 31 July, 1914, Asquith told Randall Davidson, the Archbishop of Canterbury, that in the event of war breaking out, Britain would not be dragged into the conflict. The next day, the King recorded in his diary that 'public opinion' was 'still dead against our joining in the war'. The Cabinet was split, with half the members being in favour of maintaining the nation's neutrality. Asquith and Sir Edward Grey, the Foreign Secretary, had to threaten to resign to force Cabinet to agree to honour its pre-war undertaking to France to safeguard shipping in the Channel. According to the Prime Minister, Lloyd George in particular was 'against any kind of intervention in any event.'

Then, on 3 August, Germany invaded Belgium. When news reached London, the mood changed instantly. Germany and Britain had signed a treaty guaranteeing Belgian neutrality. German violation of this pledge triggered the despatch of an ultimatum to Berlin, calling for immediate German withdrawal. Unless the Kaiser and his government acquiesced to the British demand by 11pm on 4 August, the two countries would be at war. Theobald Bethmann-Hollweg, the German Chancellor, was incredulous. 'Just for a scrap of paper', he exclaimed to Sir Edward Goschen, the British Ambassador, Britain was prepared to go to war.

Even before this, vast crowds had started to gather in London – notably outside Buckingham Palace, where they called repeatedly for the King and Queen to appear on the balcony. 'One could hear the distant roaring as late as 1.00 or 1.30 in the morning', noted the Prime Minister in Downing Street. Everyone, it

ON OUR WAY TO WAR

The front page of the *Daily Express* (above) on Wednesday, 5 August, 1914, blazons the news that Britain had declared war on Germany. The night before, Trafalgar Square had been packed with cheering crowds (right), waiting for the expiry of the British ultimatum to the Kaiser. In Downing Street, the Prime Minister was waiting vainly for a reply from Berlin that never came. Many years later, Margot Asquith, his voluble wife, recorded the scene in her autobiography. 'I looked at the children asleep after dinner', she wrote, 'before joining Henry in the Cabinet room. Lord Crewe and Sir Edward Grey were already there and we sat smoking cigarettes in silence; some went out; others came in; nothing was said. The clock on the mantelpiece hammered out the hour. We were at War.' Asquith believed that, in the absence of a German withdrawal from Belgium, British involvement in the conflict was inevitable, but he did not – like some of his colleagues – look forward to going to war. 'The whole prospect fills me with sadness', he had written earlier that afternoon. 'We are on the eve of horrible things.'

EARLY NAVAL DISASTER
Warships of the Second Battle Squadron
steam in line ready for gunnery practice off
the Donegal coast of Ireland on 27 October,
1914. This picture was taken from the
bridge of HMS *Audacious*, the Royal Navy's
very latest battleship. Shortly after the
photograph was taken, the ship struck a
German mine. Attempts to tow her back
to port failed, and she blew up and sank.
The one bright spot in the disaster was that
all the crew were saved. The Admiralty
tried to keep the sinking a secret – it was
not admitted officially until after the war.
But the luxury White Star liner RMS *Olympic*
had gone to the aid of the stricken
battleship and American passengers on
board were not to be silenced. Some of
them had even taken photographs of the
Audacious as she sank.

appeared, was now a patriot. Strolling around Trafalgar Square, the philosopher
Bertrand Russell discovered to his astonishment that 'average men and women
were delighted at the prospect of war'. In stark contrast to Russell, a pacifist, the
journalist F S Oliver was delighted at what he saw as the resurgence of true
national spirit. 'I had not conceived it possible that a nation could be born again
so quickly,' he wrote. 'This war even now has undone the evils of a generation.'

Mobilising for war

At Waterloo, crowds gathered to cheer the sailors who were being rushed to
Portsmouth to reinforce the fleet. Loud choruses of 'All the Nice Girls Love a
Sailor' and 'Rule Britannia!' rang out as the special trains slowly puffed out of the
great station, heading south.

The Navy was already prepared. Months previously, it had been decided that,
to save money, the summer naval exercises should be combined with a test
mobilisation. Some 20,000 reservists had been recalled; every battle squadron and
shore establishment was at full strength. The manoeuvres were scheduled to end

on 27 July, after which the fleet would normally have dispersed, but Winston Churchill, now First Lord of the Admiralty, and Prince Louis of Battenberg, the First Sea Lord, decided that the international situation was so threatening it would be best to keep the fleet concentrated together. Instead of being sent to their home ports, the ships were ordered northwards to Scapa Flow, ready to take up battle stations if the unthinkable happened and the nation found itself at war. They had only nine days to wait. At 11.01 pm on 4 August, 1914, a signal was radioed from the Admiralty to all British naval vessels wherever they were in the world. It read simply: 'Commence hostilities against Germany.'

The army, too, had a carefully worked-out plan. It had started with the initiation of what was termed the 'Precautionary Period' on the Wednesday before war broke out, when a signal flashed from the War Office to army commands throughout Britain and Ireland, putting them on the alert for war. Mobilisation followed on 3 August; the fateful war telegrams were despatched the following

FORCED TO RESIGN
Prince Louis of Battenberg, the First Sea Lord when war broke out, inspects naval cadets on a training ship. He had played a key part in preparing the fleet for war, but a venomous press campaign against him on account of his German birth led to his resignation on 27 October, 1914. Many thought that he had been treated unfairly. J H Thomas, a prominent Labour MP and trade union leader, wrote to *The Times* to 'express my extreme regret at the announcement that Prince Louis of Battenberg has, by his resignation, pandered to the most mean and contemptible slander I have ever known.'

continued on page 55

BRITAIN'S TROOPS GET READY

British soldiers on exercises in the south of England (above). Carrier pigeons were trained to take messages from the front line and deliver them to headquarters in the rear. As the BEF began to concentrate on the Belgian frontier in preparation for action late that August, the most pressing need was for accurate intelligence as to where the advancing Germans were and their strength. Cavalry detachments scoured the Belgian countryside, searching and probing to discover the enemy's whereabouts. The first sightings were made from the airplanes of the Royal Flying Corps – 63 of which had been flown across the Channel to act as aerial scouts. On 20 August, pilots reported that they had spotted a vast army advancing west through Louvain. The columns of marching men, they said, stretched as far as the eye could see.

In just a week, between 12 and 18 August, 1914, some 80,000 men were mobilised, equipped and shipped across the Channel to France as the British Expeditionary Force (the BEF). Here (top right), soldiers muster on the forecourt outside Euston Station in London. They landed in France at Boulogne, Le Havre and Rouen, where they were given a rapturous reception. At Rouen, where the troopships sailed right up the Seine, the banks of the river were lined with cheering French crowds. Flotillas of welcoming rowing boats struggled to keep pace with the troopships, the rowers and their passengers bombarding the Tommies on deck with gifts of fruit and flowers as the vessels passed. Much the same sort of reception took place in Boulogne, where practically all the town's inhabitants turned out to watch the troops march by to a

hastily erected camp on the cliffs just outside the town. The tents covered a solid square mile of heathland.

Many seasoned veterans, like these two soldiers (right) about to board a coast-bound train at Victoria Station, had the foresight to bring their own little luxuries with them to augment the monotony of basic rations. Others found themselves wholly reliant on bully beef and biscuit. But there was some good news to cheer them. The ban on smoking while under arms or on fatigues was relaxed and beer was freely available. The problem was that it had to be paid for in francs; soon, lines of Tommies were forming outside harassed Paymasters' tents, keen to change their money. The officers were luckier. With the exchange rate fixed at 35 francs to the pound, wine was exceedingly cheap.

'They think we cannot beat them.
It will not be easy. It will be a long job;
it will be a terrible war; but in the end we
shall march through terror to triumph.'

David Lloyd George, from a speech made at the Queen's Hall, September 1914

TO THE FRONT

British troops, newly arrived in France, wait to board a troop train that will carry them north to the Belgian border. The journey was long and uncomfortable. Each train – the aim was to despatch one every 10 minutes – consisted of 49 box-cars, which could carry 80 horses and more than 1,000 men; the officers travelled in carriages tacked on at the end. Once a train was on the move, progress was by no means plain sailing. There were long halts and delays, and even when the going was good, a strict speed limit meant that trains could not travel at more than 20mph. Few reached even half that speed. Some Tommies learned to take advantage of this; by jumping down onto the tracks, they could sprint to the front of the train, fill a mess tin with hot water from the steam engine, then rejoin their comrades waiting to brew up mugs of tea.

day. Time was tight. In little more than a week, the 80,000-man British Expeditionary Force (BEF), together with artillery, munitions, horses and other supplies, had to be shipped across the Channel to France. All this was in accordance with plans drawn up by the General Staff and agreed with its French counterparts some years before.

All over the country, troops were mustering. The Rifle Brigade was one of the first units ready to go. As its 1st Battalion marched through Felixstowe en route to Colchester, Bandsman H V Shawyer noted how he and his comrades were acclaimed by an enthusiastic crowd. 'The place was full of holidaymakers lining the pavement to see us go', he recorded. 'Most of the people couldn't do enough for us, and they were pretty loud in the doing of it, cheering, shouting, singing, waving their handkerchiefs and showering us with sweets and packets of cigarettes. Some of the young girls were even pelting us with flowers as if we were blooming Spaniards or something.'

Boulogne, Rouen and Le Havre were the BEF's chosen disembarkation ports. There, the welcome the troops got was even more rapturous. In Boulogne, the entire town appeared to have taken to the streets to greet the Tommies. The harbour wall was packed with cheering crowds. As the first troopship inched slowly towards its berth, the enthusiasm reached such a pitch that one over-excited elderly Frenchman fell in. He was quickly fished out, none the worse for wear.

INTO ACTION

It was no small achievement to ship the BEF across the Channel without a single casualty being incurred. All the soldiers were kitted out with rifles, bandoliers and pouches for their small-arms ammunition, and iron rations (emergency food consisting of a tin of corned 'bully' beef, a few biscuits, tea and sugar) to keep them going until they reached camp in France. Kitchener had penned a final message to them, which they all had to carry in their pay books. 'You are ordered abroad as a soldier of the King to help our French comrades against the invasion of a common enemy…'. The message ended with the simple but stirring injunction to 'Do your duty bravely, Fear God, Honour the King.'

No sooner had the BEF assembled in France than it was rushed north to take up positions to the left of the French Fifth Army, close to the Franco-Belgian frontier. By 24 August, it was ready for action – which came sooner than anyone had anticipated. In accordance with Germany's Schlieffen Plan, the bulk of the German armies were surging westwards through Belgium, aiming to sweep round the British and French and on into the heart of France. General Joffre, the French commander-in-chief, reacted immediately, ordering a general advance on his left flank to rebuff the German hordes.

It all sounded straightforward enough, but the reality was very different. Forming up ready for battle in and around the gloomy Belgian mining town of Mons, the BEF discovered that, far from advancing, the French were being forced back: the gap between them and the British was widening by the hour. General Sir John French, the British commander-in-chief, promptly issued new orders. He

FIGHTING AT MONS
British Tommies silhouetted along a ridge during the battle of Mons, close to the Franco-Belgian frontier. Starting on 23 August, it was the first major clash between the British and the Germans on the Western Front and ended with the BEF being forced back in a fighting retreat. Desperately outnumbered and outgunned, they nevertheless managed to check the German attack for a vital day, inflicting heavy casualties on their advancing foes. Such was the speed and accuracy of the BEF's rifle fire – its men were trained to fire a steady 15 rounds a minute – that the Germans believed they were up against machine guns. At home, many attributed the BEF's survival to divine intervention. The patriotic postcard (left) depicts some of the angels that, people said, had descended from heaven at the height of the battle to help the beleaguered British. Within weeks, the story had passed into popular folklore.

would fight on to maintain his positions along the Mons Canal and hold the advancing Germans in check to cover the French retirement. Little did he realise that his troops were outnumbered by more than three to one – or that the Germans would throw their whole weight into an attack the very next day.

Once the battle began, the British hung on grimly in the face of overwhelming German artillery fire. They repulsed attack after attack, before falling back to new positions to the west of the town. Then General French issued a new order – for a general retreat: it was vital to keep in touch with the French at all costs. The BEF obediently fell back, fighting every step of the way – perhaps most notably at Le Cateau, where General Sir Horace Smith-Dorrien, commanding the Second Corps, ordered his exhausted men to stand and check the German advance, giving the rest of the BEF more time to withdraw.

At bay on the Marne
Mile after weary mile, the retreat continued. It lasted for 13 days until the BEF finally halted on the River Marne. Though it took the personal intervention of Kitchener to persuade Sir John French to agree, at General Joffre's urging it was decided that the British and French would now turn on the advancing Germans, who had left their right flank dangerously exposed to counter-attack. And so, on 4 September, another great battle began. By the time it ended a few days later, the Germans were in full retreat. The weary but victorious Allies called it 'the miracle of the Marne.'

It was now the turn of the Germans to fall back. They retreated as far as the River Aisne, where they stopped and dug in on a chalk ridge that rose 500 feet (150m) above the far bank of the river. The Allies pursued them across, but were forced back. They tried attacking again two days later, but were repulsed once more, after which they, too, began to dig in.

The war of movement was almost over. Though no one realised it at the time, the trench warfare that would dominate tactics on the Western Front was about

DIGGING IN
British soldiers make their way along a communication trench, probably near Ypres, in late October 1914. By this time, fighting on the Western Front was fast approaching stalemate, as both sides feverishly dug trenches along a line stretching from the Channel through France to the Swiss frontier. Digging in, as it was termed, was the order of the day. A standard fire trench needed to be excavated to a depth of 7ft to 8ft (2.5m) and the sump running along the bottom covered by wooden duckboards.

A parapet of beaten earth crowned the trench on the side facing the enemy, with a similar one at the rear. The soldiers manning the trench stood on a firestep, made of earth, sandbags or wood, to peer over the parapet and observe and shoot at the enemy positions. Trenches were never dug straight. Instead, they had a series of bays facing the enemy with traverses running at an angle to the bays. The intention was to lessen the effect of a shell bursting in a trench and also to make it harder for enemy attackers to fight their way along it.

to begin. In fact, in certain sectors of the front, digging in had started even before the battle of the Marne. The tactical stalemate that followed was to prove virtually unbreakable; though no one yet imagined that the war would last so long, the deadlock was to continue until 1918.

The race to the sea

Before the stalemate developed, the Germans had one last card to play: they tried to outflank the Allies to the left. Bitter fighting flared along the open flank between the River Marne and the Channel, spreading through Picardy and Artois and on into Flanders. It was, so both sides proclaimed, a 'race to the sea'. The BEF, which that October was transported from the River Aisne up to Flanders, was in the thick of the fighting. It was centred on the Flemish city of Ypres.

By the time the fighting came to an end that autumn, with both sides settling into trenches for the winter, the BEF that had shipped out to France in August had been virtually wiped out. The Kaiser had dismissed it as 'a contemptible little army', and yet Britain's comparatively small force of highly experienced regular soldiers had played a vital part in stopping the German advance. The terrible cost was that most men of the BEF had been killed or wounded.

KEEPING IN TOUCH
Sorting the post to the BEF at the Military Post Office in London was more than a full-time job. Letters from home were eagerly awaited by the men in France, as were parcels containing tasty titbits of food, cigarettes and other items – many of them sent by complete strangers. A Company Quartermaster in the King's Liverpool Regiment recorded the arrival of two typical consignments: 'Yesterday I drew a lot of cigarettes presented by somebody, and a pipe per man sent by the Glasgow tramway men, as well as some peppermint sweets from the manufacturers. Today again there was a supply of cigarettes and tobacco as well as a lot of tinned salmon given by the government of British Columbia. We have also socks from Princess Mary, gloves from the Archduke Michael, razors from a man in Sheffield ... surely no army has ever before been so well looked after.'

THE HOME FRONT

At home, war fever mounted, even in the absence of real information from the front. The news that the BEF had suffered two serious reverses in the space of three days did not reach the public until 30 August, a whole week after the battle of Mons had been fought. Kitchener and the War Office would rather not have released the news at all. All the newspapers had to go on were the official army communiqués, which more often than not concealed far more than they revealed.

Speculation and self-sacrifice

In the absence of hard news, people turned to speculation. There was an abundance of German atrocity stories to tut-tut over at the breakfast table, largely gleaned from tales told by the growing flood of Belgian refugees. Many gave credence to the rumour that a band of angels had descended from Heaven to save the BEF from destruction in the battle of Mons. Everyone also seemed to have an opinion as to how best to be useful in wartime. Holidaymakers were urged to put aside their golf and tennis and 'enquire in any rural village whether help is required with the harvest'. Some called for theatres, music halls and cinemas to close their doors. Later, it was decreed that places of entertainment must close not later than 10.30pm, a measure christened the 'beauty sleep order.'

Everybody preached the twin virtues of self-sacrifice and economy. There were suggestions that breweries and distilleries should be shut – the grain, it was argued, could be diverted to food production. Suttons, the seed merchants, were quick to get in on the act, advertising 'the desirability of sowing and planting every spare piece of land with such food crops as there might still be time to sew before the autumn.' Many took their advice.

The government was also quick to act, ordering the banks to remain closed for three days after the August Bank Holiday to prevent a financial panic and to give time for one pound and 10 shilling notes to be printed and distributed. These were intended to take the place of sovereign and half-sovereign coins, the minting of which was suspended for the duration of the war. It was clear that the country would need its gold. The new notes, Lloyd George assured the nation, would be as safe as the Bank of England, for 'the whole credit of the British Empire' lay behind them. They were nicknamed 'Bradburys' after Sir John Bradbury, the Secretary to the Treasury, whose signature appeared on every note. Then, on 8 August, the Defence of the Realm Act – swiftly christened 'Dora' – was passed into law, giving the government sweeping new powers to assist it in putting the entire country on a war footing.

> 'Oh we don't want to lose you, but we think you ought to go! For your King and your Country need you, both need you so!'
>
> Paul Rubens, songwriter, 1914

'Your King and Country Need You'

Men from all walks of life flocked to join the colours. By the end of August, nearly 300,000 had volunteered; by December 1915, no fewer than 2,466,719 Britons

continued on page 68

FORMAL PORTRAITS

POSED FOR POSTERITY

Photographers had never been so busy as they were in August 1914. First, there were the weddings (above), as men under orders to embark for France hastened to pop the question to their sweethearts. Jewellers were gratified by the run on engagement and wedding rings. Even the Archbishop of Canterbury did his bit for romance by giving special permission for ecclesiastical offices to stay open round the clock to issue special marriage licences. He also allowed clergymen to perform marriages after the legal hour of 12 noon.

Everyone wanted their own pictorial memento in the event of the worst happening and a beloved son, brother or husband being killed, wounded or taken prisoner. The pictures here (right) are all the work of Henry Mayson, a photographer working in Keswick in the Lake District. The soldier and his wife (top) look calm, collected and ready for anything, while the boy soldier (centre) looks far too young to have been sent overseas. The two Tommies in full field uniform (bottom) are both NCOs; the one seated is a lance corporal, while the other carries an NCO's swagger stick.

FLOCKING TO THE COLOURS

They came forward in their thousands from all walks of life. Between August 1914 and December 1915, a staggering 2,466,719 men enlisted, creating the largest volunteer army in history. Many believed that the war would be short and even be fun. The poet Julian Grenfell, a regular officer and son of Lord and Lady Desborough, wrote: 'I adore war, it's like a big picnic without the directlessness'. He died of wounds in May 1915.

SMILES ALL ROUND
A crowd of happy men queue to join up at Southwark Hall, south London (left), in response to the national recruiting campaign. A patriotic song to rally the crowd would have blared out from the gramophone at this mobile recruiting station in Trafalgar Square (below), encouraging eager volunteers to register. The rush to sign up took the War Office by surprise. Lord Kitchener, the newly appointed Secretary of State for War, had appealed for 100,000 men of military age to come forward in the first instance, but in the first month of war alone, 300,000 volunteers flocked to the recruiting stations – 33,000 of them on just one day. Many men joined the new 'Pals' battalions, units linked to a specific locality or to a particular business or industry. They formed the core of Kitchener's New Army, which took to the field in 1915. By that time, with casualty lists mounting, the number of men coming forward had started to dwindle and mounting pressure was put on all eligible civilians to volunteer. Posters everywhere drove home the message and music hall stars took a leading part in the campaign. Marie Lloyd sang 'I didn't like you much before you joined the army', while Vesta Tilley chorused 'The army of today's alright'. If that was not enough, there was always the risk of being handed a white feather in the street by some woman passer-by.

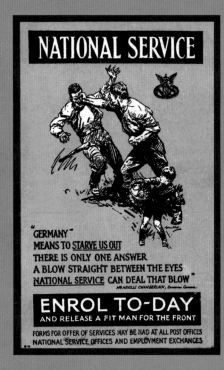

PILING ON THE PRESSURE
London street urchins (right), kitted out as soldiers with paper hats and wooden canes standing in for rifles, parade in Trafalgar Square. The purpose of their parade is spelled out in the giant poster behind them. By the end of 1914 the rate of recruitment had slowed, but men were still coming forward. These smartly dressed civilians (top) had just joined the London Scottish Regiment, while the Belfast shipyard workers (above) stand in rows behind pipers to demonstrate their readiness to rally to the cause. Some in high places called for the immediate introduction of compulsory conscription, but the government resisted the demand. Instead, a recruitment campaign called on men of military age to affirm their willingness to serve if required. It was only when this compromise failed that the introduction of conscription became politically practical.

Lord Kitchener (above left), a national hero, led the calls for men to come forward. Even those who had good reason to stay behind, because of their age or on medical grounds, were urged to enrol for civilian national service (top left), thus releasing fit young men for fighting at the front.

THERE IS STILL A PLACE IN THE LINE FOR YOU

THIS SPACE IS RESERVED FOR A FIT MAN

Will you fill it?

FIT FOR DUTY

The 'sausage machine', as it was nicknamed, worked quickly; the men here (above left), are waiting patiently for their official documentation to be processed. Like thousands of others, they were prepared to take their place in the firing line (above). Up and down the land, potential recruits were given the once-over by teams of doctors in temporary examination rooms, like this one set up in Marylebone Grammar School (left). Medical requirements were strict and a surprising number found themselves rejected as not fit to serve. Height could prove a problem. Initially, the army insisted that recruits be at least 5ft 3in tall; later, as the demand for men increased, this stipulation was eased. The War Office even raised so-called bantam units, made up solely of men below the regulation height. *The Times* explained how a short soldier had an advantage over a tall one: 'Besides lessening the size of the target for the enemy to hit, he requires shallower trenches to hide or protect him.'

GETTING READY

Recruits to the London Scottish Regiment get acquainted with their rifles under the watchful eye of a Regular Staff Sergeant-Major (above). They were lucky to be issued with guns; they were still waiting for uniforms, which, like weapons, were in short supply. The empire rallied to the mother country in her hour of need. Canada, Australia, New Zealand and South Africa all sent men to the Western Front. Detachments from the Indian Army, too, were pressed into service. These Indian soldiers (right) are about to board a troop train in Paris to take them to Flanders and the front. As the German generals prepared to attack at Ypres in autumn 1914, they told their troops that they would quickly 'finish with the British, Indian, Canadian, Moroccans and other trashy, feeble adversaries …'. Despite the cold and the unfamiliar conditions, Indian troops like these men bravely proved them wrong.

NO WAR!

Not everyone was in favour of the war and some were vehemently opposed to compulsory military service. Organisations like the Union of Democratic Control, founded in August 1914, argued for peace by negotiation. The No Conscription Fellowship, formed in December 1914, opposed attempts to introduce conscription; by November 1915, it had 61 branches spread across the country. The men depicted here (above) are attending its National Convention. The authorities were determined to clamp down on all such movements, regarding them as potentially seditious. Bertrand Russell, the leading philosopher of the day, was among those prosecuted for expressing pacifist views. In June 1916, after conscription had become law and the first conscientious objectors were being hauled before military tribunals, Russell was fined £100 for his anti-conscription activities. Trinity College, Cambridge, deprived him of his lectureship following his conviction.

had enlisted – the largest volunteer army ever raised anywhere. F B Vaughan, a steelmaker from Sheffield, was typical of the hundreds of thousands who came forward. 'My pals were going, chaps I had kicked about with in the street, kicking cans or a football, and chaps I knew very well in the city', he recollected. 'Then, when you went to the pictures you'd be shown crowds of young men drilling in Hyde Park or crowding around the recruiting office or it might be a band playing "Tipperary". The whole thing was exciting, and even in the pulpits – although it started rather shakily at first – they eventually decided to come down on the side of the angels and bless our little mission.'

Old men dyed their hair to fool the recruiting sergeants; boys barely out of school lied about their ages. All were in a hurry to get into the fight. Godfrey Buxton, a Cambridge undergraduate, recorded how he and his fellow volunteers 'were quite clear that Germany would be defeated by the 7th of October when we would go back to Cambridge'. They, like thousands of others, were to be disappointed. It took months to equip and train them. Marjorie Llewellyn, a Sheffield schoolgirl, recalled how, to their chagrin, the young men who had rushed to volunteer had been 'sent home and then sent down to the Bramall Lane football ground and to Norfolk Park, where they were drilled and learned to dig trenches'.

Joining up with Pals

Many of the volunteers joined the so-called Pals battalions, units linked to a particular locality, business or industry. Exactly who had the idea of raising them is unclear – some give the credit to Lord Derby, the biggest landowner in Lancashire and now the Director of Recruitment at the War Office – but whoever thought of it was inspired. The first Pals battalion, the 'Stockbrokers' of the Royal Fusiliers, began recruiting on 21 August. It was soon joined by others, including the Accrington Pals, Grimsby Chums, Glasgow Corporation Tramways, University and Public School Brigade, Tyneside Scottish, Tyneside Irish, Cotton Association and many more. Derby raised no fewer than four battalions of his own, so winning the title of 'England's best recruiting sergeant.' The locals on his Knowsley estate knew them as the Derby Comrades Brigade.

'We Don't Want to Lose You'

Those unwilling to come forward voluntarily came under increasing pressure to enlist. Derby himself set the tone. 'When the war is over', he declared, 'I intend, as far as I possibly can, to employ nobody except men who have taken their duty at the front.' A London firm of stockbrokers told its employees that 'the firm expects that all unmarried staff under 35 years of age will join Earl Kitchener's army at once, and also urges those who are married and eligible to take the same course.' The Parliamentary Recruiting Committee organised 12,000 meetings, 20,000 speeches and an estimated 54 million posters, leaflets and other publications to promote the cause.

Many women played an active part in shaming men into volunteering. Less than a month after the war started, Penrose Fitzgerald, a retired admiral, advised women to hand out white feathers to any able-bodied young men they saw who were not in uniform. Mrs Montague Barstow, better known to posterity as Baroness Orczy, author of *The Scarlet Pimpernel*, went one better by founding the Active Service League. Its members pledged 'never to be seen in public with any man who being in every way fit and free for service has refused to respond to his country's call'. Their efforts were

SHAMING THE 'SHIRKERS'
Women in the East End of London hoist a white feather flag from an upper window as part of their campaign to shame young men they labelled 'shirkers' into enlisting. The flag displays the words: 'Serve your country, or wear this!' The white feather campaign rapidly spread. One woman who wrote to *The Times* left no uncertainty over their stance: 'We women recognise that, as women, we have no use for the man who will not fight for his King and country. He is not fit to be the father of our children.' Advertisements reinforced the message. One, addressed to 'the Women of London', asked 'Is your "Best Boy" wearing Khaki? If not, don't you think he should be?' It concluded: 'If your young man neglects his duty to his King and Country, the time may come when he will neglect you. Think it over and then ask him to join the army – today.'

frequently misguided. Norman Demuth, who enlisted in the London Rifle Brigade, recalled how he was 'given a white feather when I was sixteen, just after I had left school. I was so astonished I did not know what to do about it. But I had been trying to persuade the doctors and recruiting officers that I was nineteen and I thought, well … I must look the part, and so I went round to the recruiting offices with renewed zeal.' A letter in *The Times* spoke for many in wondering if 'the feather-brained Ladies' would not 'be better advised to learn to nurse the wounded and thus become useful instead of offending nuisances to the community?'

THE FIRST CHRISTMAS

As the year drew to a close, people at home became more subdued; it was becoming obvious that the war would not be 'over by Christmas'. In London, though the Lord Mayor's customary Juvenile Fancy Dress Party went ahead as usual, this year the children came costumed as sailors, nurses and soldiers shouldering toy rifles. There was even a six-year-old admiral, wearing a small cocked hat and proudly sporting a little sword. Gamages, a leading London store, offered miniature field service uniforms for sale. They were complete in every detail but scaled down to fit children aged between six and 12. Hundreds were sold over the counter and by mail order.

Most people's minds were on the Tommies in the trenches. The great autumn battles, culminating in the first battle of Ypres, had finally brought the Germans to a standstill, but the casualty lists made grim reading. The armies now faced each other in a long line of trenches snaking from the sand dunes of the Belgian coast right across France to within sight of the Swiss Alps. What was left of the BEF had gone to ground in the chill Flanders wastelands. There was not much fighting going on; an ammunition shortage meant that bullets and shells were too precious to waste. Nor was the weather conducive to thoughts of offensive action, as blinding rain turned to hail and then snow. Though the generals, tucked safely behind the lines, might be debating on when and where to launch the 'big push' that would surely end the war, the minds of most of the troops were focused simply on survival.

Christmas, at least, brought the prospect of getting good cheer from home. Every soldier in the BEF received a handy metal box – a present from Princess Mary, the King's daughter – packed with cigarettes, pipe tobacco or, for the few non-smokers, chocolate. Not to be outdone, the Kaiser sent cigars, ten per man, to his troops, tastefully labelled in their boxes 'Weinachten im Feld, 1914' – Christmas in the Field, 1914. For the British there was chocolate from Cadbury and butterscotch from Callard & Bowser, together with a mountain of homemade cakes and other sweetmeats. Knitting for the troops was fast becoming a national obsession and vast quantities of socks, mufflers and other homely garments were sent across the Channel. Sometimes,

'And then we had what the English newspapers called Christmas Dinner ... cold bully beef and a cold lump of Christmas pudding.'

Private Clifford Lane, Hertfordshire Regiment

LITTLE SOLDIER
A youngster, dressed in a replica of the field uniform worn by British officers at the front, salutes smartly for the camera (left). It may well have been his Christmas present. One woman, whose 'great misfortune was to have no sons of military age', wrote to *The Times* to offer her two-year-old as a mascot to any regiment that would have him. Children featured in advertisements designed to shame men into volunteering. One celebrated recruiting poster depicted a humiliated father being asked by his children 'Daddy, what did you do in the Great War?' For older boys, there were the Boy Scouts, whose founder Robert Baden Powell proclaimed that 'Every boy ought to learn how to shoot and obey orders, else he is no more good when war breaks out than an old woman.' He concluded: 'Be prepared to die for your country ... so that when the time comes you may charge home with confidence, not caring whether you are to be killed or not.'

the recipients were less than grateful. Captain John Liddell of the Argyll and Sutherland Highlanders, writing home to his family, was critical of some of the oddities that he and his men received, especially 'the atrocity known as the heeless sock'.

The Christmas truce

As Christmas dawned, the singing of carols was heard on both sides of the barbed wire that festooned the trenches. It was probably this that triggered off one of the most extraordinary occurrences of the entire war. Along some parts of the front an impromptu unofficial truce broke out. In some places, it lasted for several days. Britons and Germans cautiously emerged from their dug-outs, crossed into no man's land and swapped greetings and gifts. Captain Stockwell of the Royal Welch Fusiliers recalled how the Saxon troops opposite presented him and his men with a barrel of beer. The Royal Welch gave the Saxons some of their plum puddings in return. Troops on both sides took advantage of the unexpected peace and quiet to mend and straighten their barbed wire, lay duckboards, pump out the water that had flooded their trenches and bury the dead.

The truce was not universal. Nor could it last. As Sergeant George Ashurst of the Lancashire Fusiliers recalled, 'the generals behind must have seen it ... so they gave orders for a battery of guns behind us to open fire and a machine-gun to open out, and our officers to fire their revolvers at the Germans. That started the war again.' Sir John French was not disposed to show the officers who had condoned the proceedings any seasonal goodwill. He reminded them that it was not their job to allow their men to strike up friendships with the enemy. Their task was to foster the offensive spirit and to win the war in 1915.

ALLIED COMMANDERS
General Sir John French, commander-in-chief of the BEF, strides across a muddy walkway in conversation with Marshal Joffre, supreme commander of the French armies, followed by some of their officers (right). General Sir Douglas Haig, who would replace Sir John French in December 1915, is on the left of the photograph. Sir John did not condone the Christmas spirit that led some British troops to fraternise with the enemy in no-man's-land in that first bitter Christmas of the war.

BOGGED DOWN

New Year 1915 began with the generals waiting for better weather and for the reinforcements they had been promised. Once Kitchener's New Army was ready to take to the field, they would break through the German lines and win the war. At least that was the plan; the appalling losses suffered at Aubers Ridge, Loos, Neuve Chapelle and Ypres would prove them wrong. Sir John French was replaced as commander-in-chief by Sir Douglas Haig, but the offensive that Haig launched on the Somme in July 1916 was even more costly than its predecessors. It was the bloodiest battle of the entire war – and was still inconclusive.

WALKING WOUNDED Two wounded British soldiers make their way towards a dressing station with a German prisoner, also wounded and walking with the aid of a stick.

IN IT TOGETHER

While some Tommies in Flanders celebrated Christmas 1914 by fraternising with their foes in no man's land, at home Asquith spent the holidays reviewing the future conduct of the war. Despite the confidence of the generals, a quick victory in France now looked increasingly in doubt. Within the Cabinet, there was growing pressure for the adoption of an alternative strategy, rather than simply shipping more and more men to the Western Front to try to break the stalemate.

Winston Churchill was the first to suggest something new. He and Lord Fisher, the First Sea Lord, had dreamed up a scheme to force open the Baltic and land an expeditionary force on its shores, just 90 miles north of Berlin. He suggested combining this with an assault on the Dardanelles in the eastern Mediterranean to open a way through the straits into the Black Sea. Churchill believed that such a blow might well force Turkey, Germany's ally since October 1914, out of the war. It would also open a direct supply route to Russia, Britain's other ally. Either scheme, he wrote to the premier, would be preferable to sending more men 'to chew barbed wire in Flanders'.

Lloyd George also favoured opening up a new theatre of war, but he argued for landing troops in Salonika in Greece. He was deeply critical of Kitchener and the War Office, which he felt had failed to get a grip on the manufacture of munitions. 'Had I not been a witness of their deplorable lack of provision', he wrote to Asquith, 'I should not have thought it possible that men so responsibly placed could have displayed so little foresight.'

'I am uneasy about the prospects of the war … I can see no signs anywhere that our military leaders and guides are considering any plans for extracting us from our present unsatisfactory position.'

David Lloyd George, in a letter to Asquith, December 1914

THE WESTERN FRONT
British Tommies and French troops march together along the main street of a small village not far behind the front line. The casual attitude of the British seems to indicate they are on the way down from the line. The troops got on well enough, despite the occasional disagreements of their leaders. Marshal Joffre, the French commander, wanted to launch a major French offensive to break through and force the German armies into headlong retreat. In his opinion, the BEF would be best employed in keeping the Germans pinned down, while the French armies bore the brunt of the battle. Sir John French, the British commander-in-chief, disagreed. He went ahead with plans for his own offensive. The battle of Neuve Chapelle was the result.

COVERING FIRE
Sweating shirt-sleeved artillerymen finally get their guns into action, after dragging them to the cliff top above Cape Helles on the Gallipoli peninsula. On paper, it had looked easy enough, but as General Sir Iain Hamilton, in command of the expedition, ruefully wrote home to Lord Kitchener, 'Gallipoli looks a much tougher nut to crack than it did over the map in your office'. This was hardly surprising, for the whole scheme had been hastily prepared. It was little wonder that, after a promising start, Hamilton's troops were forced to dig in around their beachheads.

ORDERING EVACUATION

In November, after months of stalemate and the failure of a further landing at Suvla Bay in August, Kitchener went out to Gallipoli to see the situation for himself. Until then, he had vehemently opposed any proposal for abandoning the campaign. 'I absolutely refuse to sign an order for evacuation', he had telegraphed, 'which I think would be the greatest disaster and would condemn a large percentage of our men to death or imprisonment.' The visit changed his mind. Convinced by General Sir Charles Munro, who had replaced Hamilton, and the other commanders on the spot that there was no viable alternative, he recommended pulling out. In the event, in stark contrast to the campaign itself, the evacuation was carried out skilfully with minimal casualties.

'Those damned Dardanelles'

As was his custom, Asquith did not take sides. Instead, he brokered a compromise. A fleet was to be sent to bombard the fortifications of the Dardanelles, the gateway to Constantinople (Istanbul); troops would follow, if required. The action started at the end of February, reaching a climax on 18 March, when the ships involved steamed to within a few miles of the Narrows, shelling the Turkish positions ruthlessly as they advanced.

The Turks waited apprehensively for the attack to be renewed. It never happened. Instead, Admiral John de Robeck, shaken by the losses he had incurred, decided to wait until the expeditionary force, under the command of General Sir Iain Hamilton, was ready to make a simultaneous landing. Their objective was to capture the Gallipoli peninsula and silence the Turkish guns. When Churchill tried to overrule de Robeck, Fisher supported his admiral.

The expeditionary force was not ready to disembark until 25 April, when troops from Australia and New Zealand, the ANZACs, were put ashore at what would later become known as Anzac Cove. British and French forces landed at Cape Helles. They expected a quick and easy victory, but were soon disillusioned. The Turks had used the respite they had been given well. Instead of storming ashore and advancing swiftly inland, the Allied expeditionary force found itself pinned down and confronted by newly erected Turkish defences. Trenches swiftly sprang up round the beachheads. It was the Western Front all over again.

Life back in Blighty

People at home had little to cheer. The first cracks in the industrial truce that had been agreed at the start of the war were starting to appear, as ordinary folk realised that, though they were being forced to scrimp and save, war profiteers

BOTCHED LANDING

In August 1915, General Hamilton tried to break the stalemate by landing more troops at Suvla Bay. These men (right) are British troops of IX Corps. Unfortunately, he was given the wrong man for the job. General Sir Charles Stopford was not only old and not in the best of health, but he had never commanded an army in the field. Instead of following instructions to 'push on rapidly', he delayed his advance even though, at least initially, he met little opposition. The delay gave the Turks the time they needed to rush reinforcements to the scene.

seemed to be doing very nicely out of the conflict. Prices were rising as the cost of living increased inexorably. By the beginning of 1915, food prices were 20 per cent higher than they had been six months earlier. Staples like potatoes, milk and butter doubled in price – 'the true patriot who can afford it will eat asparagus, not potatoes', the government advised – while the cost of sugar rose by a staggering 163 per cent, largely because it had to be imported.

The General Federation of Trade Unions complained that 'pallid and unappetising brisket' was now selling at 9d a pound, twice as much as before the war. Fish, too, shot up in price – so much so that the Roman Catholic Archbishop of Westminster gave his flock permission to eat meat on fasting days. The authorities preached the virtues of so-called 'meatless days' and urged people to substitute margarine for expensive butter. The King set an example by ordering the flowerbeds at Buckingham Palace to be dug up and growing his own vegetables. He also took what became known as 'the King's pledge' – to give up drinking alcohol for the duration of the war. Food manufacturers chimed in with their own helpful suggestions. 'Everyone has less money to spend on food', ran one advertisement. 'The wise ones make nourishing Quaker Oats the stand-by … Your family won't miss expensive bacon and eggs if you serve delicious Quaker Oats.'

FEEDING THE NATION
A young boy helps his father dig up their crop of potatoes on an allotment in Dulwich, south London (left). With food getting more expensive, the government began by appealing for voluntary restraint and encouraging people to eat less. Following a poor wheat harvest in North America in 1916, bread in particular was in short supply. It was not until April 1917, when Lord Rhondda became Minister of Food, that bread supplies were regulated and the price of a loaf controlled. All sorts of other controls followed; by the end of the war, 85 per cent of all the food consumed by the nation was bought and sold by firms controlled by the government and 94 per cent was subject to price control. For some, state intervention could not come soon enough. The women below are protesting against a massive increase in the price of milk, which doubled in 1916.

Tax is good!

Not to be outdone, the manufacturers of Bovril, the celebrated beef-extract drink, proclaimed that taking just a teaspoonful of their beverage before every meal would reduce daily food consumption by a fifth. People certainly needed to make economies as taxes and duties were increased on everything from beer, spirits and tobacco to sugar, coffee, cocoa and matches. An advertisement for Murray's Mellow Mixture urged people to pay up and keep on smoking: 'Don't stop smoking because tax on tobacco has increased. It is your duty to the State to keep on smoking. The Chancellor increased the duty on tobacco to give smokers an opportunity of contributing towards the successful issue of the war.' In 1915, income tax went up and its payment threshold was lowered to £130 a year.

Even though wages were rising, many found it harder and harder to make ends meet. Rents soared, particularly in places where an influx of thousands of newcomers to work in the rapidly burgeoning munitions plants led to a dramatic housing shortage. In November 1915 around 20,000 tenants on Clydeside started a rent strike. For once, the government was forced into direct intervention: it rushed a Rent Restriction Bill into law, stabilising rents for working-class housing at pre-war levels. Nevertheless, over-crowding continued while the growing shortage of building materials meant that many homes became more dilapidated.

LIGHTING UP – A PATRIOTIC DUTY

Confronted with substantial increases in tobacco duty, cigarette manufacturers turned to ingenious advertising to ensure that the British public continued to smoke. This specially customised car (right) promoted Black Cat cigarettes. Players devised a series of cigarette cards (far right) featuring soldiers, sailors and airmen in the field. The cigarette makers need not have worried; by the end of the war, three to four times as many people were smoking as before war broke out.

The Tommies in the trenches found smoking an antidote to stress and boredom, while back at home, more and more women – particularly munitions workers – enthusiastically took up the habit. 'Nothing is more soothing than a nice cigarette', one Crouch End woman wrote to *Our Girls* magazine in 1915. Another wrote: 'I think it [smoking] is one of the most consoling things in the whole world, if one is in trouble and wants to think hard.' Some even argued that smoking was good for health. According to *The Lady*, 'many fashionable physicians have actually taken to recommending a cigarette or two to numbers of their fair patients as a preventative of indigestion's awful pangs.' These wounded soldiers (right) are about to take part in a cigarette race in Harrogate as part of their recuperation at a convalescent home, puffing on cigarettes lit for them by the nurses and other women keen to see them back to fitness.

For women, smoking seemed part and parcel of the new freedom that the war was bringing to them as a whole. Hair was shorter, as were skirts; the *Daily Mail* vociferously condemned one fashionable example as 'absurdly short', revealing 'the feet, and ankles and even more of the stockings'. It became commonplace, too, to see unescorted women in restaurants and even pubs. 'The wartime business girl', reported the *Daily Mail*, 'is to be seen any night dining out alone or with a friend in the moderate-priced restaurants in London. Formerly, she would never have had her evening meal in town unless in the company of a man friend. But now with money and without men she is more and more beginning to dine out.'

PLAYER'S CIGARETTES

49TH DIVISIONAL ARTILLERY.
1916

THE HOME FRONT UNDER FIRE

For some, the actual war was coming close to home. For the first time in many centuries, Britain came under direct attack by a foreign foe. On 16 December, 1914, five battle cruisers and a light cruiser of the German Imperial High Seas Fleet stealthily steamed through the dawn mists to bombard Hartlepool, Scarborough and Whitby along the North Sea coast. In the space of 30 minutes, more than 1,500 shells were fired and 127 civilians killed. In Scarborough, the victims were either killed instantly, as in the case of one 14-month-old baby boy, or died later of their wounds. In Hartlepool, the first reported casualty was Hilda Herseley, a 17-year-old seamstress who was caught by the bombardment on her way to work. Some were lucky to escape with their lives. The *Scarborough Pictorial* recorded how one commercial traveller, having been woken by the sound of the shelling, 'hurriedly dressed and gathered his bags together, and had just got outside the door when a shell came through the wall and blew to fragments the bed which he had vacated only a few minutes before.'

To add insult to injury, the raiders slipped away, back into the mists from which they had emerged. Though the Admiralty assured people that any military damage the Germans had inflicted was 'insignificant', a howl of protest arose at the inability of the Navy to bring the enemy vessels to battle. It transpired that neither the Grand Fleet, stationed at Scapa Flow, nor the battle cruiser fleet, based at Rosyth, had been able to steam south fast enough to engage the foe.

'The first shot went at eight o'clock prompt. We were in bed asleep. But you can bet we were all soon up. Just around our house, hundreds of windows were smashed and two houses were blown to nothing next door to us.'.

Wright Bottomley, Scarborough resident, December 1914

Attack from the air

People began wondering what other horrors might be coming their way. Thomas Livingstone, a bookkeeper from Glasgow, had no doubts. 'German plans for smashing up Britain are made', he wrote in his diary in early January 1915. 'They will do it with Zeppelins and submarines, end of the month, so they say.' Sure enough, on 19 January, the first-ever air raid on Britain took place. Two

Zeppelins – the LZ- 2 and LZ-3 – bombed Great Yarmouth and King's Lynn in
Norfolk, killing two people and injuring 16. Livingstone described it as a 'German
"murder" raid,' adding acerbically 'of course the airship got away'.

The next month, in response to the British naval blockade, Germany declared
the waters around Britain to be a war zone. All shipping in British waters now ran
the risk of surprise U-boat attack. The British objected that refusing to give a
warning before launching an attack was a clear breach of international law. So
too, they said, were the Zeppelin raids which, though sporadic, grew in frequency
over the next months. People started to look out for what they termed 'Zeppelin
weather' – dark but fine, calm nights – suitable for staging attacks.

On 31 May, London was raided for the first time. The Kaiser had been
persuaded to lift his ban on air attacks on the British capital, though he insisted
that they must be confined to the districts east of the Tower of London. Two *continued on page 86*

BOMBARDED FROM THE SEA …

A Scarborough shop (left) shows the scars of battle after German battle-cruisers bombarded the seaside town on 16 December, 1914. It was one of a series of hit-and-run raids that the Imperial High Seas Fleet launched against towns on Britain's East Coast. Scarborough was not the only one hit: Whitby, Great Yarmouth, Lowestoft and Hartlepool all came under fire. Sylvia Pankhurst, daughter of the redoubtable Emmeline, was one of the 10,000 curious people who poured into Scarborough to take a look at the damage. She recorded how 'the big amusement "palaces" on the front were scarred and battered by shell-fire, iron columns twisted and broken, brickwork crumbling, windows gone. Yawning breaches disclosed the pictures and furnishings, riddled and rent by the firing, dimmed and discoloured by blustering winds and spray.'

… AND FROM THE AIR

Passers-by inspect the damage inflicted by attacking German Zeppelins in Bartholomew Close, in Central London, while workmen clear the debris and repair the sewers. Airship attacks began in January 1915, striking first at Great Yarmouth and King's Lynn. The first attack on London came on 31 May, and Zeppelins returned whenever flying conditions were right. On 13 October, four airships set off from their base in Belgium to bomb the capital in what was their most successful raid to date. LZ-15 dropped a string of bombs along the Strand, damaging the Lyceum and Strand theatres; 21 people were killed and 16 injured. The airship's commander, Kapitan-Leutnant Joachim Breithaupt, recorded how easy it was to spot landmarks like Regent's Park, the Serpentine and Waterloo Bridge from the air, despite the primitive black-out. LZ-24, carrying 30 high explosive and 10 incendiary bombs, struck at Woolwich – the arsenal there was a prime target – Croydon, Battersea and Clapham.

MONSTER CRAFT

A crowd of civilian onlookers watch in 1914 as a brand-new Zeppelin airship emerges from its gigantic hanger at Dusseldorf in western Germany. At the start of the war, the Germans possessed only five Zeppelins capable of being used for military purposes, but a crash construction programme was soon underway with a target to build 61 airships. During 1915 the Zeppelins raided Britain 19 times, starting off in January by striking at towns along the east coast, some of which had already been hit by artillery fire from the Imperial High Seas fleet. The airships moved on to attack London in May 1915, and from then on they ranged over much of the country, bringing terror in their wake. By 1917 the British defences were getting on top of the Zeppelin menace. London was ringed by 266 anti-aircraft guns and 353 searchlights with day and night-fighters on call to intercept airship attacks. Mounting losses eventually forced the suspension of Zeppelin operations. They were replaced by Gotha and Giant bombers.

airships – the LZ-37 and LZ-38 – dropped 90 incendiaries and 30 small high explosive bombs as they strafed the area between Stoke Newington and Leytonstone. Nine people were killed and 32 others injured.

Rioting followed in the affected areas, as people of supposed German origin were targeted by the mob. People were outraged by the bombings, especially since, at that time, there seemed to be no effective means of defence against aerial attack. It was not until September the following year that a German airship was finally brought down in flames by a British fighter plane. The pilot, Lieutenant William Leefe Robinson, was promptly awarded the Victoria Cross for gallantry. Another airship was downed the following month.

The Zeppelins returned time and again, spreading their attacks to other parts of the country. They got as far north as Edinburgh and as far west as Liverpool. Some people demanded that savage reprisals should be threatened against their crews. No less a personage than churchman Henry Wace, the Dean of Canterbury, demanded 'an authoritative statement that we shall make it an indispensible condition of peace that representatives of the persons responsible for Zeppelin raids should be delivered up to our Government for public execution.'

CRASHING FROM THE SKIES
Sentries guard the remains of LZ-31 (right), commanded by airship ace Heinrich Mathy and brought down at Potter's Bar, Middlesex, on 2 October, 1916. Mathy, who jumped from his vessel before it hit the ground, initially survived but died within minutes. The woman owner of a local dressmaker's shop recalled spotting the Zeppelin as it descended. 'A very long way off,' she wrote, 'was what looked like a huge ship, very high up and smothered in flames, a really wonderful but frightening sight with the blaze all orange and yellow, blowing and billowing about, all the while slowly descending until it was out of sight.' It was its slow rate of climb that proved to be the airship's Achilles heel; British air defences were also becoming stronger and better organised.

Zeppelin crash sites were a magnet for curious visitors. This crowd (above right) – momentarily distracted by a low-flying airplane – gathered in a field in Essex to view the remains of LZ-33, which crash-landed in September 1916 after being badly damaged by anti-aircraft fire. The German crew set the airship on fire to stop its secrets falling into British hands. The 20 survivors than surrendered to a single police constable, who was promptly nicknamed 'Zepp' by his colleagues.

'... something should be done to wrest from the Germans the supremacy of the air which at the present time they seem to enjoy.'

Lord Oranmore and Browne, House of Lords, 1916

THE SHELL SCANDAL

Nor were things going any better in France, where the BEF went into action at Neuve Chapelle on 10 March, 1915. Initially, the Germans were taken by surprise, but then the attack bogged down. This was largely the fault of a breakdown in communication between the troops in the front line, their reserves, the commanders in the rear and the artillery supporting the attackers in the trenches.

Generals French and Haig, commander of the First Army which had carried out the attack, and their subordinate generals quickly found a scapegoat. The commander-in-chief lost no time in bombarding the War Office with complaints about lack of ammunition. Haig railed against the munitions workers at home, blaming their fondness for holidays and drink for the shortage. 'The best thing, in my opinion, is to punish some of the chief offenders', he wrote to Leopold de Rothschild. 'Take and shoot two or three of them, and the "Drink habit" would cease I feel sure.' It sounds exceedingly harsh today, but at the time even Lloyd George agreed with him. 'We are fighting Germans, Austrians and Drink', said the Chancellor, 'and so far as I can see the greatest of these deadly foes is Drink.'

MAKING DO

By the end of 1914, the BEF was running short of ammunition and the artillery to fire it. Sir John French noted in his diary: 'There is more delay in sending these new 9.2 guns. It is said to be caused by the Christmas holidays which the men in the factories insisted on having.' Whatever the cause, in the trenches improvisation became the order of the day. The soldiers here are filling empty jam tins with nails, tamped down with gun cotton, to make primitive bombs to be hurled at the enemy. The same tins served as ammunition for an equally makeshift trench mortar, made by ingenious engineers from a length of drainpipe soldered up at one end with a touchhole bored above it.

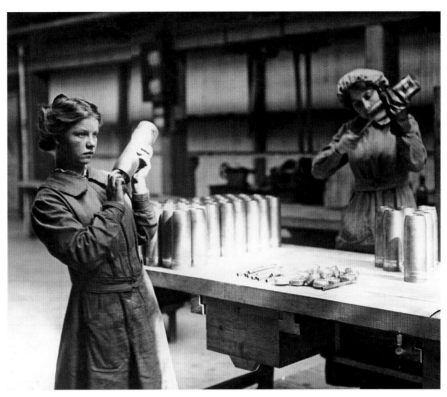

DEPENDING ON WOMEN

A government poster (above) appeals to women to come forward to join the ranks of the munitionettes, as they were called. These two women (above right) are at work in the Vickers factory in Newcastle-upon-Tyne, fitting interior tubing inside empty shell cases, ready to be filled with explosives. As 1915 dawned, the manufacture of guns and shells was lagging far behind demand. One reason for this was that thousands of skilled engineers had rushed to join the colours; another was the stubborn refusal of the trade unions to agree to unskilled labour being introduced into the armaments factories. At home, recruits to Kitchener's New Army had to drill with imitation wooden rifles, but in France, the situation was far worse. Sir John French constantly complained to the War Office that his reserves of ammunition were fast falling below danger level. Eventually, after witnessing an abortive attack, the exasperated French leaked his complaints to *The Times*. The resulting scandal was a major factor in bringing down Asquith's Liberal government; the premier formed a coalition with the Unionists to take its place.

The role of the press

Lord Northcliffe, the great press baron, blamed Kitchener. 'Lord Kitchener', he stormed in the *Daily Mail*, 'has starved the army in France of high-explosive shells.' But he immediately found out that Kitchener was sacrosanct. Overnight, the *Daily Mail*'s circulation plummeted from 1,386,000 to just 238,000 copies. In London, 1,500 indignant stockbrokers held a protest meeting to condemn 'the venomous attacks of the Harmsworth Press' on their idol, ending by burning copies of the offending newspaper on the floor of the Stock Exchange.

Lloyd George thought that Northcliffe had a point, while Asquith was also becoming disenchanted with the War Minister. Based on Kitchener's assurance that the ammunition supply was more than adequate, the Prime Minister had publicly congratulated armament workers at Newcastle-upon-Tyne for the efforts they had made and refuted the charge that they had let the country down. Yet French's protests continued. Eventually, the disgruntled commander-in-chief made his complaints public. 'I could see', he later wrote, 'the absence of sufficient artillery support was doubling and trebling our losses in men. I therefore determined on taking the most drastic measures to destroy the apathy of a Government which had brought the Empire to the brink of disaster.' He told his side of the story to Colonel Charles Repington, the military correspondent of *The Times*.

Six days later, Repington broke the news. He pulled no punches, reporting that: 'British soldiers died last week on Aubers Ridge because the British Army is short of shells.' Meanwhile, French sent two of his staff officers to London, carrying a secret memorandum outlining his complaints, with copies of all the correspondence that had passed between himself and the War Office over the preceding months. French instructed them to show everything to Lloyd George, to Arthur Balfour and to Bonar Law, the former and present leaders of the Unionist Party. French hoped that this would be enough to bring the government down.

FORMING A COALITION

In the event it was not French's revelations, damaging though they were, that led to the fall of the Liberal government. The crisis that forced Asquith into a coalition with the Unionists was sparked off by the sudden decision of Lord Fisher to resign as First Sea Lord. Tension between the admiral and Churchill over the navy's commitments in the Dardanelles had been growing for months. About the only thing they agreed on was to try to blame the luckless William Turner, captain of the transatlantic liner Lusitania for the loss of his ship. She was torpedoed by a U-boat off the coast of Ireland on 7 May, 1915, and sank in just 18 minutes. Only 761 people were saved; 1,198 passengers and crew perished. Early in the morning of 14 May, Fisher stalked out of the Admiralty intent on resignation.

As news of Fisher's departure began to leak out, Bonar Law visited Lloyd George at the Treasury and warned that he could no longer keep his restless backbenchers in check. It was more than likely, he said, that they would insist on ending the party truce in order to launch an all-out attack on the government over the conduct of the war, focusing on Churchill's alleged maladministration of the Admiralty. Lloyd George immediately saw the gravity of the situation and went to the Prime Minister. In 'less than a quarter of an hour', they agreed that a coalition government with the Unionists was the only way forward and that same evening Asquith informed Lord Stamfordham, the King's private secretary. 'After much reflection & consultation today with Lloyd George and Bonar Law', he wrote, 'I have come decidedly to the conclusion that, for the successful prosecution of the war, the Govt. must be reconstructed on a broad and non-party basis.'

With the agreement of his Shadow Cabinet, which he called together the following day, Bonar Law accepted Asquith's offer, but he made two provisos.

LUSITANIA – SURVIVORS AND VICTIMS
Survivors of the *Lusitania* disaster make their way along a street in Cork, still in shock from the experience (below left). Some of the victims were buried together in a mass grave in County Cork (right). The sinking was greeted with consternation in both Britain and the USA; the front page headline below is from the *New York Herald*. US public opinion was particularly outraged – the USA was not yet a combatant in the war, yet many of those who lost their lives were American citizens. The Cunard transatlantic liner had sailed despite an official warning from the German Embassy in Washington that the ship would be entering a war zone and passengers embarked at their own risk. She was torpedoed by a German U-boat off the Irish coast early in the afternoon of 7 May, 1915, and in just 18 minutes vanished beneath the waves taking 1,198 souls with her.

The last minutes of the vessel were confused to say the least. Fannie Morecroft, a stewardess, recalled how the passengers were 'running around like a bunch of wild mice'. She managed to escape the sinking liner in the last lifeboat to be launched. Captain William Turner, the vessel's captain, also survived to report that he believed a second torpedo had sunk his ship. Kapitan-Leutnant Schweiger, commander of the U-boat, put the explosion down to 'boilers, coal or powder.' The inquest jury in Ireland had no doubt as to who was responsible. It brought in a verdict of wilful murder against the crew of the submarine and the imperial German government.

First, Churchill would have to leave the Admiralty. And second, Lord Haldane, the Lord Chancellor, would also have to go: the Unionists had never forgiven Haldane for stating before the war that he regarded Germany as his 'spiritual home'. Both men were out. Despite fervent pleadings to be allowed to stay on at the Admiralty, Churchill was fobbed off with the sinecure position of Chancellor of the Duchy of Lancaster. Balfour took his place at the Admiralty, while Bonar Law became Colonial Secretary. Haldane retired to the backbenches. Lloyd George was appointed the head of a newly created Ministry of Munitions. Arthur Henderson, the Labour leader, became President of the Board of Education. John Redmond, leader of the Irish Nationalists, refused to serve, but Sir Edward Carson, leader of the Ulster loyalists, became Attorney-General. In all, there were 12 Liberals, eight Unionists and one Labour representative in the coalition Cabinet, plus Kitchener, who stayed on as Secretary of State for War.

Churchill did not stay in his new position for long. That autumn, when he learned that he would not be part of the new War Council, he resigned and went to command a battalion of Royal Scots Fusiliers on the Western Front. Major Jock

McDavid witnessed the former minister's arrival in the trenches. 'Out of the first car', he recollected, 'came this well-known figure dressed in a long, fine-textured waterproof, wearing a poilu helmet and a Sam Browne belt holster with a revolver stuck well into it … the second car … was piled high with luggage of every description. To my horrified amazement, on the very top of all … was a full-length tin bath. What the hell he was going to do with all this I couldn't think.'

Forging the guns

The most demanding of the challenges that the new government faced fell to Lloyd George at the Ministry of Munitions. He started off with just two secretaries in a tiny office equipped with two tables and a single chair. By the end of the war, the ministry's headquarters staff alone numbered more than 25,000, managing around 20,000 'controlled establishments' and the 15 giant National Projectile Factories, the same number of National Filling Factories and the four National Cartridge Factories that Lloyd George had ordered to be built from scratch.

Lloyd George let nothing stand in the way of boosting the armaments supply by the fastest possible means. The Munitions of War Act, passed in July 1915, gave him the power to do anything he thought necessary to expand armaments production. His ministry had absolute priority over supplies of fuel, power and

transport, and over land for building new factories. He could also order existing factories to produce for the government and, if necessary, bring them under state control.

The task faced by Lloyd George was daunting. It was not only guns, mortars, shells, machine guns – the War Office had ordered 26,000, but only 5,500 had been supplied – and rifles that were lacking. The army needed 70,000 hand grenades a day and was receiving just 2,500. To fortify a single mile of the Western Front demanded 900 miles of barbed wire, 6 million sandbags, 1 million cubic feet of timber and 360,000 square feet of corrugated iron. The response to the challenge was magnificent. By the time Lloyd George took over at the War Office in July 1916, the number one priority of industry had at last become the mass-manufacture of weapons to enable the army to beat the Germans in the field. It was a far cry from the business-as-usual attitude that had hitherto prevailed.

Labour unrest

Before the formation of the coalition, ministers had brokered an industrial truce in an attempt to put an end to strikes and labour disputes for the duration of the war. Most importantly, trade unions agreed to allow the unskilled to do the work of the skilled, to abandon restrictive practices and to accept compulsory arbitration to settle disputes. The proviso was that things would return to normal after the war. As a quid pro quo, an excess profits tax, designed to stop employers making too much money out of supplying war materials, was eventually introduced. But there remained some legal, if nefarious, ways of mitigating the tax, as many canny businessmen discovered. It looked well enough on paper, but not everyone toiling at the coalface, in the

COALITION MEMBERS
Unionist leaders Sir Edward Carson (above left) and Andrew Bonar Law (above right) cross Whitehall on their way to the House of Commons in August 1915. Both became ministers when Prime Minister Asquith formed a Coalition government, Bonar Law serving as Colonial Secretary and Carson as Attorney-General. Bonar Law had been instrumental in bringing about the formation of the Coalition that May. Alerted by General Sir John French to the BEF's lack of ammunition, and alarmed by Lord Fisher's sudden resignation as First Sea Lord, he voiced to Lloyd George a growing concern about his ability to keep his backbenchers under control. He and Lloyd George agreed that only the formation of a truly national government could solve the growing political crisis and Asquith concurred. Carson's tenure of office was short-lived. He resigned in October in protest at the failure of the Allies to send military assistance to help Serbia. The following year, he put himself at the forefront of opposition to the way in which the war was being conducted and played a pivotal role in bringing about Asquith's resignation.

'I would say that ultimate victory or defeat in this War depends on the supply of munitions which the rival countries can produce and with which they can equip their armies in the field.'

David Lloyd George, House of Commons, June 1915

shipyards and in the engineering works was prepared to go along with the deal. In February 1915, the first serious strike of the war broke out on the Clyde when 5,000 engineers downed tools in protest at some American workers being taken on at higher rates of pay. That July, 200,000 miners in South Wales downed tools in protest against the attempt to impose a national pay settlement on them.

In December, with the Clydeside engineers again threatening trouble, Lloyd George rushed north to appeal personally to their shop stewards not to take industrial action. In a mass-meeting on Christmas Day, attended by 3,000 men, he was howled down. The ruffled minister returned to London in a rage. Frances Stevenson, Lloyd George's secretary and mistress, recorded in her diary: 'D says that the men up there are ripe for revolution … He is convinced there is German money up there.' Though this dispute was eventually settled – the government assured the militants that their jobs were secure and that their traditional privileges would be restored after the war – there were more strikes to come.

'We want to work'

Many women were eager to do their bit and take the place of the hundreds of thousands of men who had volunteered to join the fighting services, but things were slow to get off the ground. In March 1915 the government launched a registration scheme for women prepared to work for the war effort. Almost 79,000 women immediately came forward, but only 1,800 of them found jobs.

Many felt that this was simply not good enough. That July, Mrs Pankhurst and her fellow suffragette Millicent Fawcett organised a massive 'Women's Right to Serve' rally. Some 30,000 demonstrated in Hyde Park in London, carrying banners emblazoned with slogans such as 'We Demand the Right to Work', 'Shells Made by a Wife May Save a Husband's Life' and 'Women's Scissors Will Cut The Red Tape'. They were pushing at an open door. The nation was ready for change.

Many women, primarily from the upper and middle classes, went into nursing. The number of military nurses rose from 2,600 in 1914 to more than 18,000 by the end of the war, with a further 74,000 serving in VADs (Voluntary Aid Detachments). The society beauty Lady Diana Manners was one of them. After training as a VAD at Guy's, she persuaded her parents, the Duke and Duchess of Rutland, to turn part of Arlington House, their palatial London home, into a hospital for the wounded. Agatha Christie, another VAD, became a dispenser in a hospital pharmacy. She put the knowledge she gained of poisons to good use when she turned detective writer after the war.

Women took over from men in offices, on the trams, buses and railways, in shipyards and engineering plants and on the factory floor. Many found work in the rapidly expanding armaments industry, filling shells with high explosives and shrapnel. They were swiftly dubbed 'munitionettes'. Lord Selborne, the President

TAKE COVER
A 1915 government poster, featuring comparative silhouettes of enemy and Allied aircraft, tells people what to do 'should hostile aircraft be seen'. To signal an imminent attack police constables careered through the streets on bicycles, blowing whistles to attract attention and wearing large placards with the words 'Police Notice. Take Cover.' Boy Scouts and members of Church Lads' Brigade sounded their bugles to signal the all-clear.

MOVING WITH CARE
Women in an armaments factory gently steer loaded shells from the factory floor. From the time the government set up the Ministry of Munitions, the number of women working in the munitions industry steadily increased. In June 1915 the Woolwich Arsenal employed only 195 women; by July 1916 the figure had risen to 11,000 and to more than 250,000 a year later. Though reasonably well-paid, working conditions were hazardous. In addition to the risk of accidental explosions, many women contracted TNT poisoning in which the chemicals in the explosive attacked the red corpuscles in the blood and vulnerable body organs, such as the liver. Toxic jaundice was another hazard and the faces of women suffering from it turned bright yellow.

of the Board of Agriculture, set up the Women's Land Service Corps, which eventually became the Women's Land Army. *The Times* gave its blessing to such changes. 'Even if many of the posts formerly held by men which women are now filling are for the duration of the war only, and will have to be yielded up should their original holder return safe and sound, they will have tested women's capacity in a way that may have a lasting effect on women's work in the future.'

It was not all plain sailing. Some women met opposition from their male co-workers, who resented their arrival in the workplace. And with so many cooks, maids and housekeepers leaving domestic service for better-paid war work, many middle and upper-class women struggled to run their homes. 'Neither my Mother, sister or myself had ever done any serious housework or cooking of any kind, so it was an entirely new experience to be confronted with meals to cook and rooms to clean', one officer's wife recalled. 'It required an entirely new mental adjustment.'

The coming of conscription
Manpower and how best to mobilise it was one of the most critical problems facing the coalition government. As voluntary recruitment slowed down and the casualty lists rose, military demands for more and more men constantly increased. In the spring, Kitchener had committed the country to creating a 70-division army on the Western Front, but, month by month, it seemed more and more unlikely that the target would ever be met without compulsory military service. The politicians were divided. Many Unionists and some Liberals – most notably Churchill and Lloyd George – favoured conscription. So, too, did King George

continued on page 100

WOMEN AT WORK

Before the war, women were most commonly employed in domestic service. Now, they stepped forward to fill the shoes of the hundreds of thousands of men away at the war. By the end of the war, the number of women in paid employment increased from 5.9 to 7.3 million. They were not paid as much as the men they replaced and some of them faced considerable male hostility. One Lancashire tram conductress recalled how male passengers sometimes simply refused to show her their tickets.

BRAVE NEW WORLD
Women took over from men in all sorts of jobs and surprised many by their abilities and strength. This young woman delivering coal (left) seems well up to the physical demands, as do the two porters carrying luggage at Marylebone Station (below right). Initially the government was slow to realise the part women could play on the home front, but they soon came to appreciate how they could help to win the war. The poster (below left) appeals for volunteers to join the Women's Land Army. By September 1916, the Board of Agriculture calculated that 57,497 women had registered in 30 counties, although only 28,767 of them were currently employed. Ploughing, milking, hoeing and harrowing competitions were organised to show farmers what women could do. After one competition in Hertfordshire in July 1917, *The Times* wrote of 'the land women, bronzed, freckled and splendidly healthy' clearing ditches, loading carts with manure and harnessing horses. On average, land volunteers earned 3d to 4d an hour for an eight-hour day – less than an unskilled farm labourer, but with board and lodging provided.

NATIONAL SERVICE
WOMEN'S LAND ARMY

"GOD SPEED THE PLOUGH AND THE WOMAN WHO DRIVES IT"

APPLY FOR ENROLMENT FORMS AT YOUR NEAREST POST OFFICE OR EMPLOYMENT EXCHANGE

ALL KINDS OF JOBS
There seemed no limits to what women could do if given the chance. These photographs show women window-cleaners setting off to work in Piccadilly (top), female mechanics probing the internal workings of a truck's engine (above left) and women workers on the factory floor of an engineering shop (above right). The land girl (opposite page, top) is working on a farm in Surrey, while the forestry workers (bottom) are enjoying a laugh during their lunch break in Epping Forest. The popular patriotic poetess Jessie Pope celebrated their achievement in her poem 'War Girls', published with other poems in her *Simple Rhymes for Stirring Times*. The final lines of 'War Girls' ran:

'There's the motor girl who drives a heavy van,
There's the butcher girl who brings your joint of meat,
There's the girl who calls "All fares please!" like a man,
And the girl who whistles taxis up the street.

Beneath each uniform,
Beats a heart that's soft and warm,
Though of canny mother-wit they show no lack;
But a solemn statement this is,
They've no time for love and kisses.
Till the khaki soldier boys come marching back.'

who wrote to Asquith that, though he trusted 'we shall not be obliged to come to compulsion', he was 'interested to see it has been advocated in the H of C this evening by one of your late whips, who has been at the front for ten months!!!'. Many Liberals opposed it just as fervently, some on conscientious grounds and others, including Reginald McKenna, who had succeeded Lloyd George as Chancellor, because they doubted whether the country could afford its cost.

The Prime Minister prevaricated. After the failure of the BEF's autumn offensive at Loos in September 1915 – during the battle, the British, following the German example, employed poison gas for the first time – he eventually nerved himself to change the commander-in-chief in France, replacing French with Sir Douglas Haig. He also took away some powers from the over-extended Kitchener by bringing General Sir William Robertson (who had been French's Chief of Staff) back to the War Office and appointing him head of the Imperial General Staff. Now, he faced the army's insistent demand for 35,000 new recruits a week.

At first, Asquith compromised. Lord Derby devised the so-called Derby scheme, under which all men of military age were urged to attest that, if called upon to join the colours, they would do so. Out of 2.2 million eligible single men, about 840,000 came forward; around 1.35 million married men attested, trusting Asquith's promise that single men would be called up before them. Parliamentary pressure mounted on the beleaguered premier until two Military Service Acts – one in March and the other in May 1916, extending the call-up to married as well as single men – made universal conscription law.

THE EASTER RISING

It was while the controversy over conscription was reaching its climax that the government found itself facing another major crisis. On Easter Monday, 1916, some 2,000 Irish National Volunteers, abetted by members of the Irish Citizen Army, rose in armed rebellion in Dublin and proclaimed an Irish Republic. They took over the General Post Office in Sackville Street as their headquarters, where they were promptly besieged.

Though British intelligence had warned that a rising was likely, Asquith and his colleagues seemed taken by surprise. Duff Cooper, a young civil servant in the Foreign Office, recorded how they got the news. 'During the morning', he wrote in his diary, 'they brought us over a telegram which Birrell [the Irish Chief Secretary] had received from Ireland and which he hadn't been able to decode because his secretary was away and no one else knew where the cipher was!' Cooper concluded acerbically: 'It really seems amazing that when things of this kind are going on in Ireland Birrell should be unable to decipher his own telegrams …'.

Reinforcements were despatched to crush the rebellion, which itself had got off to an inauspicious start. The ship the rebels were counting on to supply them with arms had been sunk off the Kerry coast a few days before, while Sir Roger Casement, a former British diplomat who had made his way to Germany to plead the Irish cause, had been arrested soon after being landed back in Ireland from a

continued on page 104

THE IRISH REBELLION
British regulars snipe at Nationalist rebels from behind a hastily erected barricade of beer casks near the Dublin quayside (right). The British administration was initially taken by surprise, but troops were rushed to the scene to nip the uprising in the bud. The Nationalists were outnumbered and outgunned; they had hoped for German aid, but the promised arms never came. Michael Collins (top), seen here in the uniform of a general in the Irish Volunteers, and Eamon de Valera (above) were two of the rebel leaders who lived to fight again. Others were not so fortunate and were executed by British firing squads.

THE AFTERMATH

Dubliners view the remains of buildings destroyed by British artillery fire during the Easter Rising (left). After the rebellion had been suppressed, the government authorised a policy of savage repression. Fifteen of Sinn Fein's leaders were court-martialled and shot, while martial law was imposed throughout the south of Ireland. Sir Roger Casement (above), who had gone to Germany to plead for help for the Irish Nationalist cause, returned to Ireland on the eve of rebellion and was arrested soon after. He was imprisoned in the Tower of London, tried for treason at the Old Bailey and hanged in Pentonville Prison. He is seen here on his way to the gallows. Asquith deputed Lloyd George to try to broker an Irish settlement, but despite his most persuasive efforts, the 'Welsh wizard' failed to reconcile the two sides. When Lady Scott, widow of the explorer and confidante of the Prime Minister, asked what else could be proposed, Asquith replied: 'They have nothing to suggest but despair.'

German U-boat. Nevertheless, it still took the British six days and much bitter fighting to force the insurgents to surrender. Some 450 Irish were killed and 3,614 wounded; on the other side, the death toll was 116 British soldiers and 16 members of the Royal Irish Constabulary.

Reprisals were immediate and savage: 15 of the ringleaders were summarily executed by firing squad. Among them were Patrick Pease, the Republic's provisional president, and the wounded James Connolly, who had to be propped up on a chair to be shot. Some 3,000 rebels and supposed sympathisers were arrested, 1,867 of them ending up in prison. Casement was hung for treason in Pentonville jail. British rule in Ireland continued for the rest of the war.

THE BIG PUSH ON THE SOMME

The Irish rebellion was a most unwelcome distraction, for the entire attention of the government – and ultimately of the nation – was fixed on the great offensive that General Haig was preparing to launch on the River Somme, along a 20-mile stretch of the Western Front. It was the long-awaited 'big push' and this time, the government was assured, it would be successful. Backed by more guns than ever before, the BEF would smash through the German defences and win the war.

Originally, Haig had planned the battle with Marshall Joffre as a joint Franco-British effort, which was why the Somme had been chosen rather than Flanders, which Haig would have preferred. The plan was for the two Allied armies to launch an all-out assault on the German positions on the Somme, with the British attacking to the north and the French to the south of the river. But in February 1916 the Germans began a massive and sustained attack on the French positions at Verdun. Months of intensive fighting had drawn off most of the troops that Joffre had intended for the Somme: by the time battle was joined, only six French divisions were free to fight with the British.

In truth, Haig was not too worried by the reduction in the French contribution. He wanted to win a decisive British victory. The BEF had been massively reinforced by Kitchener's New Army, which was finally, so it was felt, ready to take to the field. Haig was in command of nearly a million men and had the chance to put his offensive plans into effect. An awesome artillery bombardment would precede the initial assault, ceasing only when the troops were ready to go over the top. The attacking foot-soldiers were told that the sheer

BIG GUNS
The 39th Siege Battery artillery in action during the battle of the Somme (right). In the week before the battle, more than a million shells were fired on German positions in a preliminary bombardment. The rolling rumble of the guns could be heard across the Channel. And yet this massive bombardment failed in both its primary objectives, which were to cut the barbed wire entanglements protecting the German trenches and to destroy the machine-gun nests that formed the backbone of the enemy defence. When Britain's Tommies went over the top, they found both were still intact.

INTO THE STORM
British soldiers go over the top during the
battle of the Somme (below), which began
on 1 July, 1916. On the first day they were
cut down in their thousands by German
machine-gun fire. Half of the first wave
were killed within 30 minutes of going over
the top. By evening, the BEF had suffered
57,470 casualties; of 13 villages targeted,
three had been taken in an advance of less
than a mile. On 14 July a second attack
further south along the river met with some
initial success, but a third thrust at the end
of the month was a total failure. Worsening
weather eventually forced Haig to call a halt
on 19 November. The British had advanced
just seven miles and lost 419,654 men, of
whom 131,000 had died on the battlefield.

'The first line all lay down and I
thought they'd had different
orders because we'd all been told
to walk. It appears they lay down
because they'd been shot and
either killed or wounded. They
were just mown down like corn.'

Private Reginald Glenn, York and Lancaster Regiment, 1916

fury of the barrage would obliterate any defences confronting them, annihilate the enemy artillery and smash to smithereens the machine gun nests that festooned the German lines.

Over the top

The 'big push' began on 1 July, 1916. Promptly at 7.30am the sound of officers' whistles rang along the trenches as thousands upon thousands of men started to scale the assault ladders. Private Albert Andrews, serving in the Manchester Regiment, recorded the countdown: 'The orders came down: "Half an hour to go!" "Quarter of an hour to go!" "Ten minutes to go!" "Three minutes to go!" I lit a cigarette and up the ladder I went.' They began moving forward into no-man's-land, advancing in line and at a steady pace, precisely as instructed. John Andrews, another private in the Manchester Regiment, recorded that he carried with him 'a rifle and bayonet with a pair of wire cutters attached; a shovel fastened on my back; pack containing two days' rations, oil sheet, cardigan, jacket and mess tin; haversack containing one day's iron rations and two Mills bombs; 150 rounds of ammunition; two extra bandoliers containing 60 rounds each, one over each shoulder; a bag of ten bombs.' Weighed down by loads like this, the troops probably would have not been able to move faster even if they had tried.

It soon became clear that, despite Haig's hopes, the preliminary bombardment had failed in its objectives. In many places, the barbed wire was not cut, while the

GAS, BOYS, GAS!
Soldiers of the Machine Gun Corps man their Vickers weapon wearing gas-masks during the battle of the Somme in July 1916. By this stage in the war, gas-masks were standard equipment for every soldier, but when the Germans first used gas, at Ypres in spring 1915, it took the British completely by surprise. The War Office immediately appealed to the public to make half a million gas masks at home. Harrods set up a special counter to sell the gauze, cotton wool and tape required and its staff gave demonstrations of how to put a mask together. The government aimed to send 100,000 of these home-made masks to the front within a week. Meanwhile soldiers were told to improvise by wetting a piece of cloth – handkerchiefs and socks were favourites – to tie over the mouth and nose until the gas clouds passed. Before long the British were using gas against the Germans, too.

COPING WITH THE WOUNDED
A dressing station on the Somme packed with wounded awaiting treatment. No one had foreseen the number of casualties. Lieutenant Lawrence Gameson, a young medical officer, recalled how he 'worked for hours on end without respite; at the crude dressing tables, at men grounded on stretchers, at men squatting or sitting'. The walking wounded were the most fortunate; the seriously injured had to face agonising journeys in unsprung ambulances jolting over the endlessly shelled roads back to hospitals behind the lines. Sergeant Tom Price remembered how he and six other wounded men were 'put on a Ford ambulance van with rubber tyres, hard wheels. I don't know which of the six of us screamed the most on that journey down over the rutted, shell-holed roads.'

German machine guns were firing to murderous effect. Then the German artillery opened fire. By the end of the day, the BEF had suffered 57,470 casualties, of whom 19,240 had been killed or died of their wounds. There was to be no breakthrough. Instead, the battle went on and on, with Haig's troops launching attack after attack until, with the coming of the autumn rains, the slaughter was finally brought to an end on 19 November as the troops once again bogged down in the mud. In four-and-a-half months of savage fighting, the longed-for great advance had been limited to just seven miles.

At home, the casualty lists, when they appeared, made heartbreaking reading. Marjorie Llewellyn, a Sheffield schoolgirl, recorded that 'there were sheets and sheets in the paper of dead and wounded ... It was a very, very sad time – practically everybody was in mourning. People were in deep black, the men, if they couldn't wear black, wore black armbands as a mark of respect. The city was really shrouded in gloom ... and nothing seemed to matter anymore.' Asquith himself was closely affected. Raymond, his eldest son who was serving in the Grenadier Guards, was shot down and killed leading his men over the top.

THE MEN IN CHARGE

General Sir Douglas Haig (right, centre) pictured visiting some of his troops in December 1915, shortly after he replaced General Sir John French as commander-in-chief of the BEF. Both Haig and the newly appointed chief of the Imperial General Staff, General Sir William Robertson (on the far left of the picture), believed that the war could be won only by defeating the German army on the Western Front. And that meant confronting them in battle, even if thousands upon thousands of young men would be shot down in the process. At the end of the first day of fighting on the Somme, Haig was relatively content with the way the battle had gone. He wrote in his diary that evening that his casualties could not 'be considered severe in view of the numbers engaged and the length of the front attacked'.

THE WELSH WIZARD

David Lloyd George, Kitchener's successor as Secretary of State for War, on a visit to the Somme in September 1916 (right). His hat is raised to acknowledge the cheers of the troops as he emerges from a captured enemy dug-out. That same month, Lloyd George gave an interview to an American journalist in which he discounted any possibility of a negotiated peace. Britain, he declared, would fight on to 'a decisive finish', however long it took and however great the sacrifice.

Nor was there any other good news to cheer people up. On 31 May, the two great fleets had finally clashed in the North Sea at the battle of Jutland, but far from winning a Nelsonic victory, as everyone had expected, the Royal Navy ended up losing more ships than the Imperial High Seas Fleet. Before turning tail and making for home, the Germans managed to sink three British battle cruisers, four armoured cruisers and eight destroyers. The Germans lost one battle cruiser, an old pre-Dreadnought battleship, four light cruisers and five destroyers. 'Heavy and Unaccountable British Losses', ran the headline in the *Daily Express*, echoing Admiral Sir David Beatty's comment as two of his battle cruisers blew up in quick succession. 'Chatfield', he said to one of his officers, 'there seems to be something wrong with our bloody ships today.'

THE FLEETS CLASH

On 31 May, 1916, for the one and only time in the entire war, the British and German battle fleets clashed – in the North Sea at Jutland. On paper, the Royal Navy's Grand Fleet, commanded by Admiral Sir John Jellicoe, was vastly superior, but in the opening stages of the action the Germans inflicted substantial losses on the British battle-cruiser fleet. The picture (above) shows the *Queen Mary* blowing up and HMS *Lion* suffering heavy damaged. The battle ended with the Germans retiring back to port and both sides claiming victory.

ASQUITH FALLS

The coalition government began to crumble. In June, Lloyd George pressured the Prime Minister into appointing him Secretary of State for War in place of Kitchener, who had drowned while on a diplomatic voyage to Russia when HMS *Hampshire* struck a mine. At the time Margot Asquith wrote presciently in her

'I saw that I could not go on without dishonour or impotence, or both; and nothing could have been worse for the country and the war.'

H H Asquith, in a letter to a friend shortly after his resignation

diary: 'We are out: It can only be a question of time now when we shall have to leave Downing Street.' Her husband's tenure of office would indeed come to an end that December when he was forced to resign.

Meanwhile, Lloyd George found himself unable to exert much power over the generals – Robertson, as Chief of the Imperial General Staff, had supreme strategic authority – and grumbled that he was little more than a butcher's boy, rounding up men to be slaughtered. With Unionist support, he urged Asquith to set up a new, small War Committee to take over much of the responsibility for running the war. He would be its chairman. Before finally agreeing, Asquith demanded it was made clear that he retained 'supreme and effective control of War policy'.

The two men agreed that they could live with the compromise, but then something happened that made it unworkable. For months the press, particularly *The Times* and *Daily Mail*, had been almost unremittingly critical of Asquith. The very day after the concordat with Lloyd George, *The Times* returned to the attack. Someone – possibly Lloyd George himself – had leaked the terms of the agreement. Asquith had had enough. In December 1916 he wrote to Lloyd George demanding that he, not Lloyd George, be chairman of the War Committee: 'Unless the impression is at once corrected that I am being relegated to the position of an irresponsible spectator of the War, I cannot possibly go on.'

The fight was on. Asquith had already announced his intention of reconstructing the government. Lloyd George now made it clear he would not serve in an administration on Asquith's terms, and the Unionists – some more reluctantly than others – backed him. With the Unionists against him and his own party divided, Asquith lacked the support to carry on. He resigned.

The King called the party leaders to a conference, chaired by Arthur Balfour, who was accepted as being impartial. His conclusion was that it was impossible for Asquith to form a new government. Bonar Law was ready to try to do so, if Asquith was prepared to serve under him. If not, Lloyd George should be given the chance. After consulting Liberal colleagues, Asquith declined. Accordingly the King summoned Lloyd George to Buckingham Palace. Within 24 hours, he had formed a new coalition government and Asquith was gone – for good. So the country ended the year with a new leader. One thing, though, was certain. The war would go on. It would be fought, said Lloyd George, to 'a knock-out blow.'

OVERTHROWN
Herbert Henry Asquith (above), pictured in 1916 shortly before his enforced resignation as Prime Minister. He had led the Liberal government brilliantly since 1908, but by this time, the 64-year-old premier was no longer at the height of his powers. As the war news went from bad to worse, his seemingly laid-back conduct of affairs was considered by many to be dilatory. Under him, the Coalition government was unsettled and unstable; he also had to face constant press criticism – notably from Lord Northcliffe. As the political crisis around Asquith's premiership neared its climax, Northcliffe was deterred only at the last minute from sanctioning a *Daily Mail* leading article headed 'Asquith: A National Danger'. After the resignation, Asquith wrote to a close friend: 'I have been through the hell of a time for the best part of a month, and almost for the first time I begin to feel older. In the end, there was nothing else to be done, though it is hateful to give even the semblance of a score to our blackguardly Press.' He never held office again.

BRITAIN
BATTLES ON

The year 1917 was the bleakest of the war. In an attempt to starve Britain into submission, Germany resumed unrestricted submarine warfare: in April alone, 545,282 tons of British shipping were lost. As supplies at home began to run short, the Ministry of Food urged Britons to cut back voluntarily on what they ate. Food queues grew longer and prices soared. Nevertheless, most Britons were ready to see things through. The Admiralty was forced to adopt a convoy system in an attempt to defend merchant shipping against U-boat attack. Then the United States of America joined the war on the Allied side: things must surely get better.

THE YANKS ARE HERE Two US soldiers fire at a German machine-gun nest in September 1918, as infantry advance through what remains of the Argonne Forest in northeast France. By this time, the final German attempt to win the war had failed and they were in full retreat.

IN THE BALANCE

In 1917, Britain's two main allies were in a parlous state. Russia was teetering inexorably towards revolution, while in France the failure of General Robert Nivelle's all-out assault on the Chemin des Dames ridge that April led to widespread mutinies. Nivelle, a hero of Verdun, had replaced General Joffre as commander-in-chief of the French armies in December 1916. Now it was Nivelle's turn to go. In May, the French government called upon the more cautious General Philippe Petain, the other great hero of Verdun, to take overall command and restore order among the ranks. Petain promised his war-weary troops that there would be no more futile, costly offensives. 'We must wait', he said, 'for the Americans and the tanks.' In April 1917, the USA had finally joined the war on the Allied side, but it would be many months before its troops could play a significant part in the struggle.

Like Nivelle, Haig scorned such passivity. At the end of July, he launched another supposedly war-winning offensive – this time in Flanders, centred on the tiny village of Passchendaele. Again, the men paid a terrible price. Then, in March 1918, the Germans launched their own offensive. Following the Russian Revolution in October 1917, Russia's new rulers negotiated their own exit from the war, freeing up thousands of troops from the Eastern Front to reinforce the German armies in the West. Haig's troops were driven into retreat. Massive assaults on the French followed, forcing them back in turn. For a while, it seemed to some as if the Kaiser might, after all, win the war.

Eat less food

Thomas Livingstone, still keeping his diary in Glasgow, recorded on 10 January, 1917, that 'the War Loaf is official'. To save grain, the amount of white flour in bread was reduced and substituted with other grain or potato flour. People complained about the new loaf, known by many as 'Government Bread,' but they still ate it. In an attempt to check bread consumption, the new Ministry of Food urged Britons to heed the advice of a character called Mr Slice O' Bread. Cutting out 'waste crusts', the poster advised, would save 48 million slices of bread a day; similarly, the ministry calculated that if every person in the land saved a teaspoon of breadcrumbs a day, the total saving would amount to 40,000 tons a year. Following the King's example, loyal citizens were urged to take what was christened the Householder's Pledge to voluntarily reduce bread consumption by a

SAVING FOOD AND RATIONING
The message of the poster is clear – a direct appeal to the nation to save bread. At first, rationing was voluntary; in February 1917, Lord Davenport, the newly appointed Minister of Food, urged people to restrict themselves to no more than four pounds of bread, two-and-a-half pounds of meat and 12 ounces of sugar per week. In April, Davenport was replaced by Lord Rhondda, who in February 1918 instituted an official rationing system. It was tested out in London and the Home Counties, and following success there, rationing was rolled out across the entire country in July. Each household had to register with a retailer, who was supplied according to the needs of his customers. The weekly allowances were one-and-a-half pounds of meat per person, four ounces of butter or margarine and eight ounces of sugar. Women were allowed four pounds of bread a week; men got seven. Children aged less than six got half the meat ration, though adolescent boys and men involved in heavy labour got extra. The number of customers in restaurants was restricted and all had to hand over coupons with their orders.

'We've no unpatriotic joint,
No sugar and no bread.
Eat nothing sweet, no rolls, no meat,
The Food Controller said.'

Aelfrida Tillyard, *Invitation Au Festin*, 1917

FRESH FROM THE OVEN

In France, army bakers (right) display newly baked loaves fresh from a mobile bread oven. At home, people were encouraged to cut down on bread consumption so that troops at the Front had sufficient, and by early 1917 food shortages were starting to bite: the women and children (below) are waiting for a South London soup kitchen to open. The German U-boat campaign to starve Britain into submission was reaching its height. Eventually, the government set up National Kitchens to provide cheap meals for the needy. The first was opened by Queen Mary in May 1917. The Queen herself served the first meals, but one elderly customer did not realise who was serving him. 'The fact that it was the Queen must have been pointed out to him by the crowd outside', an observer reported, 'for shortly afterwards he returned, edged his way back to the serving-counter, and solemnly waved his hat three times at her.'

WAR IN THE CLOUDS
High in the sky above the Western Front, a helmeted and goggled German observer prepares to drop a bomb from the rear cockpit of a two-seater biplane. Air power started to come of age as the war progressed. At first, airplanes were unarmed and limited to reconnaissance duties. Soon, however, dedicated fighter planes – scouts as they were termed at the time – and bombers began to emerge from the mushrooming aircraft factories. Planes regularly strafed artillery positions or troops on the move below and the two sides vied for air supremacy. Sir Hugh Trenchard, commander of the Royal Flying Corps, which became the Royal Air Force on 1 April, 1918, committed his pilots to a 'relentless and incessant offensive' to drive the Germans out of the skies. Losses were high: in 1917, it was reckoned that the average life span of a newly trained fighter pilot posted to the Western Front was between 11 days and three weeks.

quarter and to 'abstain from the use of flour in pastry'. The campaign even had a badge – a purple ribbon with the slogan 'I eat less bread' – while schoolchildren throughout the land were encouraged to learn the campaign song.

The problem was that bread was the staple food, especially since meat was becoming far too costly for most ordinary folk to buy except on special occasions. In April, *The Observer* reported that queues for bread and potatoes at Edmonton in North London were so long that the police had to be called to regulate them. By December, according to *The Times*, queues of a thousand people or more were commonplace. Small wonder that there was a resurgence of industrial unrest. In March 1917, many munition workers came out on strike, followed by engineers at Rochdale. By May, the unrest had spread to 48 towns, with 200,000 workers idle.

It was not until 1918 that Lord Rhondda, who had succeeded Lord Devonport as Minister of Food, finally brought in official rationing. The scheme was piloted in London and the Home Counties before being introduced nationally in July. The new rations were enforced by police. One man from Mitcham in south London, charged with illegally shooting a deer, pleaded in mitigation: 'It's a job to live on these meat rations. I must have something for my children.' He was heavily fined, as was a woman from Dover, who fed bread and milk to her 14 dogs.

Disaster in Silvertown

The arrival of the 'War Loaf' was not the only bad news to report. Glaswegian Thomas Livingstone recorded in his diary that there had been a 'great munitions factory disaster near London'. The catastrophe happened on 19 January, 1918, in Silvertown in the East End. As firemen tried to put out a fire in a chemical plant there, 50 tons of TNT, an extremely powerful high explosive, suddenly detonated.

ACES HIGH

Pilots, observers and ground crew of No 1 Squadron, Royal Flying Corps (RFC), pose for the camera. One pilot (right foreground) is holding a beagle – the squadron's mascot. By the time of the battle of Arras in April 1917, RFC pilots had shot down some 200 enemy aircraft. Everyone, from Lloyd George downwards, admired the airmen greatly; the premier dubbed them 'the knighthood of the war, without fear and without reproach'. They were certainly brave. For one thing, when they flew they were not equipped with parachutes – officially, the reason was that the parachutes of the day were too bulky to fit into a fighter's cockpit, but a secret report of the Air Board revealed another reason: 'It is the opinion of the Air Board that the presence of such an apparatus might impair the fighting spirit of pilots and cause them to abandon machines which might otherwise be capable of returning to base for repair.'

A large part of the factory was instantly destroyed, together with many buildings in nearby streets. It was the biggest single explosion ever recorded in the capital. In all, some 70,000 homes were damaged, 73 people were killed – 69 instantly and four later in hospital – and more than 400 were injured. The bodies of those closest to the explosion were never found. The noise resounded right across the capital. Elizabeth Fernside, a housewife in Fulham in West London, reported: 'The noise was so terrific that I thought the Huns had dropped a surprise packet. There are … great cracks and gaps in the roads, people three miles off were blown out of their houses and were running about, seeking a place to shelter.'

Death from the skies

Contrary to popular rumour, an official enquiry concluded that the Silvertown explosion was accidental and was not caused by a German bomb. But at the end of May, the enemy returned to the skies over Britain for real and this time, rather than Zeppelins, they were flying new, twin-engined Gotha G-4 bombers capable of carrying a 1,000-pound payload. Flying out of bases at Ghent in Belgium, they struck first at Folkestone in Kent, dropping 23 bombs and killing 95 people, a number of whom had been waiting in a food queue outside a shop. The bombers moved on to London, which quickly became their main target. The city was raided by day and by night. The first raid, on 13 June, 1917, resulted in 162 deaths and

TAKING SHELTER

Two volunteers (left), clutching mugs for tea, stand in the exit of a YMCA dugout, erected as an air raid shelter in a London street. Government policy did not stretch to providing individual family shelters, but some, like this family in south London (above), built their own. Most people took shelter as best they could under railway arches, in church basements and crypts, and in the cellars of private and public buildings; in Knightsbridge, for example, Harrods threw open the vast man-made caverns under the store to people seeking safety. Thousands of Londoners sheltered in the Underground. At the height of the attacks, in autumn 1917, up to 300,000 people a night were taking refuge in Underground stations. When the air raid alarm was raised, the crowds were at times prone to panic. One St John's Ambulance Brigade Officer noted: 'Everyone runs at once ... People arrive in a state of excitement which changes to hysteria when the guns begin to fire.' By the time the Germans called off their bombing campaign a year later, due to mounting losses, they had flown 397 missions; 24 Gothas were shot down and 37 lost through accidents.

432 injuries, mainly in the area around Liverpool Street Station. Another daylight raid that same month killed 158, including 18 children at a school in Poplar, and caused near panic throughout the East End.

The government was quick to take action. An iron ring of anti-aircraft guns and searchlights was thrown around the capital, while Royal Flying Corps fighters were recalled from France to bolster the defences. Nevertheless, bombers still got through. Maroons – a type of firework – were fired to raise the alarm as bombers approached, and people rushed to take refuge in cellars, under railway arches, in foot tunnels beneath the Thames and in the London Underground. All waited anxiously for the sound of bugles being blown by Boy Scouts and Boys' Brigades to signal the 'All Clear'. The upsurge of public outrage at the continued attacks led King George V to change the name of the Royal dynasty from the German-sounding Saxe-Coburg-Gotha to plain patriotic Windsor.

Preparing for Passchendaele

Lloyd George's mind was not on the air offensive. It was focussed on what was going on in France, where Haig was advocating the launch of another all-out offensive. Flushed with the British success at Messines in June 1917 – where, after a year's careful preparation, 19 enormous mines literally blew a hole through the German defences – Haig argued that his forces were more than capable of breaking out of the Ypres salient, advancing into open country, forcing the Germans into full-scale retreat and finally winning the war.

The carnage that the Second Army, under the command of General Herbert Plumer, had inflicted on the Germans at Messines was impressive. Captain Martin Greener, a Company Commander in the Royal Engineers, recorded how 'the earth seemed to open and rise up to the sky. It was all shot with flame. The dust and smoke was terrific.' Rifleman Tom Cantlon, of the King's Royal Rifles, recalled that 'None of us had ever seen anything like it ever. It was just one mass of flames. The whole world seemed to go up in the air.' The attack, *The Times*

reported, was a 'brilliant British success'. The King was quick to congratulate the troops. 'Tell General Plumer and the Second Army', he wrote to Haig, 'how proud we are of his achievement, by which in a few hours the enemy was driven out of strong entrenched positions held by him for two-and-a-half years.'

Lloyd George was not convinced by Haig's new proposals. The new offensive, he believed, could easily turn into another Somme. Summoning the commander-in-chief before the War Cabinet, the premier told Haig bluntly that incurring heavy casualties in yet another inconclusive battle would have 'disastrous effects on public opinion'. It would be preferable to wait for the Americans and for the French armies to recover from their own failed offensive, or to send troops to support the Italians in their bitter struggle against the Austrians. Anything would be better than gambling with hundreds of thousands of lives 'merely because those directing the war can think of nothing better to do with the men under their command'. But eventually Haig got his way and the War Cabinet, albeit reluctantly, authorised him to continue preparing for his attack.

THE BATTLE OF PASSCHENDAELE

Over the next month, reinforcements moved inexorably towards the jumping-off points for the attack, taking full advantage of the cafés in places like Poporinghe along the way. Night after night, the Tommies crowded into them, consuming mountains of eggs and chips and drinking gallons of cheap white wine. It cost just a franc a bottle. Then, on 16 July, Haig started the preliminary bombardment. He had mustered no fewer than 2,299 guns – one to every five yards of the front – to smash the German defences. During the two weeks the barrage lasted, the British artillery fired four times as many shells as it had during the prelude to the Somme.

The constant drumming of the distant guns could just be heard in London, 120 miles away, where the War Cabinet met over dinner. It decided, somewhat late in the day, to allow the offensive to start, but with a major proviso. According to Sir Maurice Hankey, the Secretary to the War Cabinet, it was not to be allowed to 'degenerate into a drawn-out, indecisive battle of the Somme type'. If that happened, 'it was to be stopped and the plan for an attack on the Italian front would be tried'. But nothing could stop the offensive now.

On 31 July, at 3.50am, the soldiers of the Fifth Army, commanded by General Sir Hubert Gough, went over the top. It all started deceptively well – but ended badly. By the end of the first day of battle, the attack had stalled on the German

defences. Then it started to rain and the downpour continued without a let-up. The next month was to be the wettest in Flanders in living memory. The ground that the troops were expected to advance over rapidly turned into a swamp. Every stream turned into a torrent and every ditch into a watercourse. The trenches filled with water faster than the Tommies could bail them out. The massive artillery barrage had not helped as the shellfire had destroyed the intricate local drainage system, so helping to create a muddy morass.

The conditions were indescribable, particularly for the wounded waiting to be rescued from the battlefield. Sister Calder, a nurse at a casualty clearing station, recalled how the 'boys', as she and the other nurses referred to them, 'were in a shocking state, because so many of them had been lying out in the mud before they could be picked up by the first-aid orderlies. Their clothes were simply filthy. They didn't look like clothes at all. We had to cut them off and do what we could.'

Bogged down in mud

Undeterred, Haig ordered the attack to continue. On 16 August, Gough's men went over the top again, but although they succeeded in taking the village of Langemarck, fierce German counter-attacks – and the rain – prevented further gains. The Fifth Army had now lost 3,420 officers and 64,586 other ranks since 31 July. Gough appealed to Haig to call off the offensive, but the commander-in-chief was confident that his strategy was correct. General John Charteris, his Chief of Intelligence, assured him that he was killing Germans faster than his own men were being killed. Haig was also told that, once his troops managed to get onto the ridge above the little village of Passchendaele, they would find it 'as dry as a bone'. He turned to General Plumer to get him there.

Plumer was not ready to renew the attack until 20 September, when another massive artillery barrage signalled the start of yet another assault, as the Second Army men fought for control of the ridge above the Menin road. To an extent the attack succeeded – in places, the British line moved forward by up to a mile – but it did not achieve the breakthrough that Haig still believed was possible. Plumer attacked again at Polygon Wood and Broodseinde. The casualty lists grew longer. By the end of September, British losses amounted to 88,790 killed and wounded.

One more time

Haig called for one last all-out effort. The British attacked again – this time, without a preliminary bombardment in the hope that they would take the Germans by surprise. But the advancing British ran headlong into the Germans, who had been preparing to launch their own counter-attack. And the weather worsened again into the bargain. Both Plumer and Gough now appealed to Haig to halt further attacks, but he responded by throwing the Australians and then the Canadians into the battle.

At last, on 10 November, the Canadian Corps, supported by the Anzacs on their right and the Royal Naval Division on their left, succeeded in taking the ridge and the village of Passchendaele. The cost had been terrible – in the words of Corporal Baker of the 28th North-West Battalion: 'My impression was that we had won the ridge and lost the battalion.' The commander-in-chief finally decided to bring the battle to a close. He had captured a barren wilderness. After nearly three-and-a-half months of fighting, the BEF had advanced just a few miles.

continued on page 126

THE WOUNDED AND THE DEAD

Stretcher-bearers recovering casualties from the battlefield of Passchendaele near Ypres (right). Often they waded knee-deep through mud (left). For the wounded, this was just the start of a long journey. With the help of a specially laid railway (below), a workhorse hauls casualties from a field dressing station to the base hospital; from there they would be put on a hospital train and shipped back to Blighty. By August 1917 packed hospital trains were pulling into Charing Cross Station every hour. Then there were the dead to be buried. Paddy King, a young Lieutenant in the East Lancashire Regiment, recalled how he and his fellow subalterns were each ordered to take out a section of men to perform this gruesome task: 'It was an appalling job. Some had been lying there for months and the bodies were in an advanced state of decomposition and some were so shattered that there was not much left.'

Indeed, it had failed to secure all of the objectives that Haig had confidently predicted would be taken during the first day of the battle.

It was worse, some said, than the Somme. Lieutenant Guy Chapman, serving in the Royal Fusiliers, recorded being told, as his unit moved up to the front, that the earlier battle was a 'picnic' compared to Passchendaele. General Sir Launcelot Kiggell, Haig's Chief of Staff, was shocked when he finally paid a visit to the battlefield. The story goes that he broke down in tears as his car bumped towards the front, exclaiming 'Good God, did we really send men to fight in that?' One of the officers escorting him simply replied: 'It's much worse further up.'

False triumph at Cambrai

Haig, now a Field Marshal, told a frankly disbelieving Lloyd George that he had come close to breaking the morale of the German army, thanks to the vast number of casualties that had been inflicted on it. In fact, the losses were probably about equal on both sides at Passchendaele. Nevertheless, the commander-in-chief had one final card to play. Even while the battle was coming to a close, he

FIGHTING FROM SHELL HOLES
Canadian troops in a quagmire of mud slowly advance up the ridge above Passchendaele in the teeth of determined enemy resistance. Haig had thrown the Canadian Corps, under General Sir Arthur Currie, into the battle in a last-ditch attempt to take the village and the high ground above it, but the Germans were ready for them. Private Jim Pickard of the Winnipeg Grenadiers recorded his experience of one abortive attack: 'The shells were falling thick and fast, and by some sort of capillary action the holes they made filled up with water as you looked at them – or as you lay in them, for the only way we could move was to dodge from one hole to another, hoping that lightning really didn't strike twice in the same place.'

WONDER WEAPON
Soldiers ride on a Mark IV tank during an exercise. In 1917, the British launched their first mass tank attack at Cambrai, quickly punching through the enemy defences. Corporal Jack Dillon of the Tank Corps recalled: 'We got through all four German lines without any serious opposition. The tanks reached their objective quickly and when I caught up with them I found the crews sitting down drinking mugs of tea.' It was a great victory and the church bells in England were rung to celebrate it, but there were no reserves available to follow up the attack and the Germans soon recovered the lost ground.

authorised General Sir Julian Byng, commander of the Third Army, to launch yet another attack on the Germans – this time to the south at Cambrai.

Earlier in 1917, Byng had been in command of the Canadian Army Corps and won a major victory when his troops captured Vimy Ridge. He planned his new assault equally carefully. There was to be no preliminary artillery barrage to alert the enemy that his troops were about to go over the top. Instead, his men would go into action led by more than 300 tanks – some specially equipped with fascines (bundles of brushwood) to bridge the German trenches. The attack did take the Germans by surprise and the tanks breached the much-vaunted Hindenburg Line in several places. Behind them, the Third Army advanced nearly four-and-a-half miles, losing just 5,000 men. By the standards of the Western Front this was astonishing progress. It was, without question, a clear-cut victory. At home, the government ordered the church bells to be rung in celebration.

But the bells rang out too soon. With no reserves on hand to take advantage of the initial success, the British could not make their gains secure. In addition, many of the tanks proved mechanically unreliable and broke down. A fierce counter-attack by the Germans drove the British back and retook all the lost ground. By the time the fighting ended on 7 December, the BEF had suffered another 45,000 casualties. Haig's claims that enemy morale was at rock bottom had been shown to be demonstrably false.

continued on page 132

IN THE TRENCHES

The men of the BEF had hastily dug themselves into trenches for some sort of protection during the war's first winter, but by 1918 the trench system had become much more sophisticated. There was a lightly held Forward Zone, the main Battle Zone and a Rear Zone. With everyone expecting a major German attack, Haig ordered the British forces to defend their positions in depth. The question was whether there would be enough time to prepare the defences fully.

WAITING AND WATCHING British and French troops share a dug-out in a trench on the Western Front during a lull in the fighting in early 1915 (below). The BEF was to launch its first major offensive later that spring. Three years later men were still in the trenches. Here (right), one man keeps watch while his colleagues from the 7th King's Liverpool Regiment stand to at a strong point in the Forward Zone in mid-March 1918. The photograph was taken shortly before the Germans launched the all-out offensive that their commanders confidently expected would win the war before the Americans had time to arrive in strength. After Britain's serious losses of the previous year – and Lloyd George's stubborn refusal to sanction the despatch of replacements – Haig and his generals were short of men to repel the expected attack when it came. Sir Hubert Gough, commanding the Fifth Army on the Somme, where the first blows fell, had no illusions about what was coming: 'We knew we were going to be attacked in overwhelming force.' The onslaught started on 21 March, 1918. Aided by the cover of a thick morning mist, the Germans soon broke through the Fifth Army's defences.

SEEING IT THROUGH
Men of the Duke of Wellington's Regiment show the ability to sleep anywhere, as they take shelter in a shell hole after a successful advance into no-man's-land (left). Back in the BEF's front line, some Tommies brew up helpings of hot stew on a so-called Tommy cooker (top), while others snatch a nap in a cramped dugout (above). What the Tommies called all-in stew was a favourite, as were porridge and pea soup. Some trenches were far superior to others, as the 23rd Brigade found when it took over a section from the French on the River Aisne in May 1918. In the words of Lieutenant Walter Harris, detached from the Rifle Brigade to command a trench mortar battery, they were: 'The best system of corridors and dugouts I had ever seen – it must have been a great effort by the French to make such a fine underground headquarters.' Captain Philip Ledward was also impressed: 'The trenches and dugouts were in wonderful condition.'

BEHIND BARBED WIRE

German prisoners-of-war in a holding cage at Saint-Hilaire-au-Temple on the Marne (left). Haig was convinced that his attacks were wearing down the enemy. When Lloyd George visited him in August 1917, Haig arranged for the premier to be taken to visit a prisoner-of-war camp, where, he insisted, the Prime Minister would see for himself how the prisoners were exhibiting a marked 'deterioration in physique'. But before Lloyd George arrived at the camp, the prisoners were carefully sorted so that he was shown only the oldest, the most unfit and the most unprepossessing. Despite such precautions, Sir Maurice Hankey, the War Cabinet secretary who accompanied the Prime Minister on his inspection, recorded how the prisoners 'still sprang to attention as though under review by the Kaiser'.

ON THE DEFENSIVE

As the year 1917 drew to its close, there was little good news from the various war fronts to cheer up the folk back home. The one encouraging development was the British army's success in Palestine. On 9 December, General Sir Edmund Allenby's forces marched into Jerusalem, liberating the city from the Turks and bringing four centuries of Ottoman rule to an inglorious end. It was an ideal Christmas present for the war-weary nation. The government particularly welcomed the news, since the previous month it had authorised Arthur Balfour, now Foreign Secretary, to write what was to become one of the most famous letters in history. The Balfour Declaration, as it became known, pledged Britain to 'view with favour the establishment in Palestine of a national home for the Jewish people'. It was the first official recognition of Zionist ambitions by a major power.

Haig had other things on his mind. For the first time, some of the press was turning against him. *The Times*, which had previously been one of his strongest supporters, called openly for his replacement. Lloyd George would have been happy to oblige, but Haig still had powerful friends in high places. He survived, but General Sir William Robertson, the Chief of the Imperial General Staff, did not. In February 1918, the Prime Minister engineered Robertson's removal by promoting him to be the country's chief military representative on the new Allied Supreme War Council at Versailles. When Robertson refused the post – and also the chance of staying on in his current position but with reduced powers – he was sent off to take charge of Eastern Command. General Sir Henry Wilson, no friend of Haig's, took Robertson's place as head of the Imperial General Staff.

The bottom of the barrel

If Lloyd George could not sack Haig, he could at least clip his wings. 'Haig does not care how many men he loses,' the premier confided to close colleagues. 'He just squanders the lives of these boys.' Rather than give the commander-in-chief the replacements he was seeking, the Prime Minister kept as many men as he could away from the Western Front. In any event, the nation's manpower reserves were rapidly approaching exhaustion. Accordingly, the government gave priority to the navy and the air force, followed by ship-building, airplane and tank manufacture, then food and timber production. The army was bottom of the list.

To make more recruits eligible, the age limits for conscripts were lowered to 17 years 6 months and raised to 50 (55 in the case of doctors). The newspapers launched a virulent campaign against the retention of men of military age in the Civil Service, labelling government departments 'the funkholes of Whitehall'. Duff Cooper, chafing at the bit in the Foreign Office, finally abandoned his London life for the rigours of an officers' training battalion. Eventually, he was commissioned into the Grenadier Guards. Not everyone, though, was keen to see their sons going off to serve King and country. Private Reginald Backhurst, conscripted into the Royal West Kent Regiment, recalled how, on the last day of his embarkation leave before sailing for France, his mother 'followed me around the house until it was time for me to go. I got to the front door and she was crying and holding me round my knees – I was forced to drag her to the front gate.'

Looking for light relief

Yet life went on and people tried to make the best of it, even if the imposition of an entertainments tax had driven up the price of theatre, music hall and cinema tickets. Gramophone records were selling faster than ever. People in their thousands flocked to chuckle at the latest madcap silent exploits of Charlie Chaplin. In London, musicals like *Chu Chin Chow* and *The Maid of the Mountain* and revues like *The Bing Boys are Here* – with its immortal hit song 'If You Were the Only Girl in the World' – played nightly to packed houses.

Music halls and dance halls were crowded, too, as were a new social phenomenon – night clubs. In London's Soho district, more than 150 of them sprang up. They were frequently raided by the police, who had been urged to crack down on after-hours drinking, but they flourished nevertheless. People managed to get away on holiday as well, even though the trains were overcrowded and often late. Sports lovers were not so fortunate, as some golfers in Eastbourne found in February 1918, when they were heavily fined for illegally using petrol to get to the golf course. Professional football had not been played since 1915, when the Football Association gave in to newspaper calls for its suspension. With the exception of the annual Newmarket meeting, horse-racing ceased as well. Even that peculiar British institution, the annual Oxford and Cambridge Boat Race,

continued on page 138

GAS VICTIMS
Temporarily blinded by German mustard gas, casualties wait to be treated at an advanced dressing station near Bethune, during the battle of the Lys in April 1917. The photograph inspired the American painter John Singer Sargent, then serving as an official war artist, to paint his celebrated picture 'Gassed'. By 1918, both sides had built up deadly arsenals of gas shells employing various types of gas. So-called Green Cross shells contained phosgene, a lung irritant that was 16 times more lethal than the chlorine gas used when the new weapon made its first appearance on the Western Front in 1915. Yellow Cross shells contained mustard gas, which, as well as severely burning the skin, had a terrible effect on the eyes. Soon, its victims were blind, helpless and in agonising pain. Furthermore, this insidious gas took up to ten days to disperse.

ROAD TO RECUPERATION

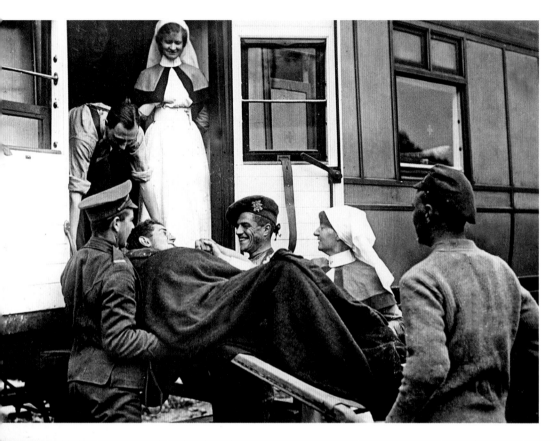

A wounded Tommy is carefully placed on board a hospital train, ready to head back to London. As the war dragged on, many Tommies hoped to receive what they called a 'Blighty' wound – one that was not too serious, but bad enough to get them invalided home. 'You thought', wrote Corporal Clifford Lane of the Hertfordshire Regiment, that 'a Blighty wound was the most fortunate thing that could happen to you.' Many of the troops recuperating from their wounds back in Britain were from around the empire. The Indian troops below are being cared for in Brighton Pavilion, which was converted into a military hospital early in the war. British-ruled India – which at that time encompassed Pakistan and Bangladesh – mobilised 827,000 troops and contributed £100 million to the escalating cost of the conflict. In return, Edwin Montagu, Secretary of State for India in the Coalition, promised that greater powers of self-government would be granted after the war. Thousands of nurses were needed to care for the men. By 1918, there were more than 18,000 military nurses, plus some 74,000 members of the VADs (Voluntary Aid Detachments). The nurses riding on the roundabout (right) are taking part in an event laid on for the wounded at Sidcup in September 1917; two of their charges are mounted on the horses behind them.

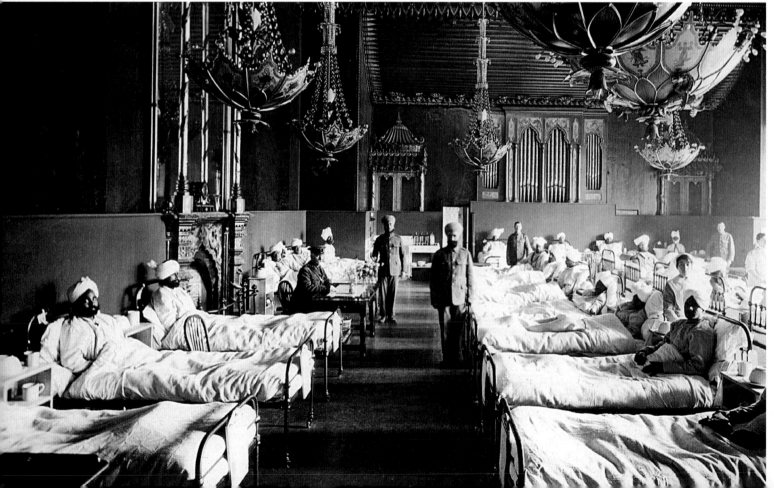

was abandoned. Only boxing seemed to flourish, for somewhat obvious reasons. As *The Times* described it, 'Here are something of the ingredients of war – blood and sweat and struggle, the cunning manoeuvring for blows and the taking of them cheerfully … here is the courage of the battle in miniature.'

'With our backs to the wall'

In France, for the first time since 1915, Haig and the BEF were preparing to take the defensive. In part this was due to a shortage of fighting men and an agreement with the French to take over more of the front, but the main reason was Haig's awareness that, with Russia out of the war following the Bolshevik Revolution, massive German reinforcements were heading west. The German High Command had come to a momentous decision. It would gamble everything on a final bid for victory before the Americans arrived in strength. By March 1918, they had amassed 191 divisions on the Western Front, faced by 178 on the Allied side.

The big question was where and when would the Germans strike. The answer came on 21 March when Ludendorff, the German Quarter-Master General, and Hindenburg, the German army's supreme commander, unleashed their forces on the Fifth Army. Under the command of General Sir Hubert Gough, the Fifth Army was holding a long stretch of the front line between Cambrai, St-Quentin and La Fere. Gough's men were assailed along a 50-mile front in an all-out German effort. Vastly outnumbered, they buckled under the ferocity of the attack.

Supported by more than 6,000 guns, the Germans attacked at 9.40am. By the end of the day, they had advanced up to eight miles and Gough had ordered a general retreat. This opened up a gap between his forces and Byng's Third Army, on the British left. The Germans were quick to take advantage of the opportunity. By 23 March, they had punched a 40-mile-wide hole in the British lines and were pouring forward into open country.

> '**We are fighting a very powerful foe, who, in so far as he has triumphed, has triumphed mainly because of the superior unity and concentration of his strategic plans.**'
>
> Lloyd George, House of Commons, April 1918

As Gough fell back across the Somme, Haig anxiously conferred with Petain. The German intention seemed clear: to drive the British and French apart and then advance up both banks of the River Somme, forcing the BEF back on the Channel ports and the sea. Haig appealed to Petain for support, but the latter was not convinced. He expected to be attacked at any moment in Champagne and had instructions from the French government to protect Paris at all costs. He would give Haig what help he could, but must follow his orders, even if that meant losing contact with the battered British armies.

Haig was thunderstruck. He noted after the meeting that Petain struck him 'as very much upset, almost unbalanced'. When they heard what Petain had proposed, so were the British and French governments. At a hastily convened meeting at Doullens on 26 March, it was agreed that the situation was so desperate it required emergency action. The pugnacious Marshal Ferdinand Foch would be appointed to supreme command of the Allied armies. Meanwhile, the fighting raged on. The determined German thrust was eventually halted just short of Amiens, but they were by no means finished. Ludendorff turned on the British in

TEMPORARY HALT
British soldiers man a makeshift barricade in a street in Bailleul in a vain attempt to check the advancing Germans. Despite their best efforts, the town fell a few hours later as the German Sixth and Fourth Armies desperately attempted to crush the British as they retreated through Flanders. Haig's troops finally managed to check the enemy advance, but not before General Herbert Plumer's Second Army had been forced to withdraw from Passchendaele, the scene of so much sacrifice less than a year before. At home, the setbacks rekindled national determination. *The Times* advised: 'Be cheerful, face facts and work; attend volunteer drills regularly; cultivate your allotments; don't exceed your rations; don't repeat foolish gossip; don't listen to idle rumours and don't think you know better than Haig.'

Flanders, driving them back to the gates of Ypres. It was, Haig thought, the supreme crisis of the war. On 11 April, he issued a special order of the day to the BEF. 'There is no other course open to us but to fight it out', he exhorted his weary men. 'With our backs to the wall and believing in the justice of our cause each one of us must fight on to the end. The safety of our homes and the freedom of mankind alike depend on the conduct of each one of us at this critical moment.'

THE TIDE TURNS

There was no denying that the British had suffered terribly in the German onslaughts. Some were near the end of their tether. Lieutenant Frank Warren, of the King's Rifle Corps, recorded how the troops under him were 'gaunt and weary, unwashed and with eight days' growth of beard … they obey orders mechanically, but sink fast asleep when opportunity offers.' Captain Thomas Westmacott, marshalling traffic across a vital bridge over the River Somme, concurred. 'Towards midnight, about 500 men passed me on the bridge, deadbeat and hardly able to walk', he recalled. 'I shouted out "What battalion is that?" and a man I knew answered out of the darkness "It is what is left of the 17th Brigade".'

But things were about to change for the better. Though the exhausted British Tommies could not know it, the tide of battle was starting to turn against Ludendorff. Further attacks on the BEF were repulsed as all along the line the troops managed to stand firm, resisting German attempts to exploit their initial successes. The advancing enemy was finally running out of steam. Ludendorff had failed to take Amiens. He had failed in Flanders, where Plumer had managed to blunt the German attack. Now, like a floundering whale, he threw his troops against the French in an attempt to break through to Paris. They came within 40 miles of the French capital, before being halted again on the Marne. Then, on 7 July, the French turned and counter-attacked, aided by the Americans, who were now arriving in France at the rate of 250,000 a month. Ludendorff cancelled a projected offensive in Flanders. By 7 August, the Germans had been forced back almost to where they had started.

At home, the nation had rallied round the government, recognising that this was a time of national peril. Strikes practically ceased and productivity soared as the factories and munitions plants worked around the clock to churn out more than enough shells, guns and tanks to make up the British losses. Reinforcements were rushed to France. In Parliament, Lloyd George triumphantly trounced Asquith as the former premier attempted to censure him for misleading the House about the BEF's strength at the start of the offensive. Asquith also had to face wild accusations levelled against him during an extraordinary libel case brought by Maud Allen, a celebrated dancer of the day, against Pemberton Billing, an eccentric

THE VICTORS AND THE VANQUISHED
Brigadier-General Campbell, commander of the 137th Brigade, addresses his troops from the bridge over the St-Quentin canal at Riqueval (left), which they captured from the Germans on 29 September, 1918. The 137th Brigade was part of the 46th Division, which by the end of the day had taken 70 guns, more than 1,000 machine-guns and 4,200 prisoners. The demoralised Germans were by now surrendering en masse. Arthur Pick, a captain in the Leicestershire Regiment, recorded how he and his men entered an enemy trench and 'found the occupants unarmed, all their belongings packed up and ready to be marched back'. The British soldier (above) is offering a captured German a drink of water from his canteen, as other dispirited prisoners of war look on.

right-wing Independent MP. In making his defence against Maud Allen's suit, Billing alleged that Asquith and his wife Margot were among 47,000 sexual 'perverts' listed in a German 'Black Book' and that they were being blackmailed into sabotaging the British war effort. It was all obvious nonsense, but the jury acquitted Billing in just half an hour.

Forward to victory

Haig judged that the moment had come to strike. The pessimists at home – Sir Henry Wilson, chief of the Imperial General Staff, and Winston Churchill, whom Lloyd George had brought back into the Cabinet as Minister for Munitions, were among them – might believe that the war would drag on into 1919 and even 1920. The commander-in-chief knew better – and this time he was right.

On 8 August, the BEF smashed through the German lines at Amiens, advancing eight miles and taking 15,000 prisoners. 'It was', said Ludendorff, 'the black day of the German army.' Hammer blow followed hammer blow as, between 21 August and 25 September, the British repeatedly attacked all along the Somme. As one victory succeeded another, the Germans fell back in disorder, their resistance crumbling with each new blow. Ludendorff hoped that his battered troops would be able to regroup behind the massively fortified Hindenburg Line and hold on for the winter, but on 29 September Haig's troops stormed across the Canal du Nord and broke through the German defences. At last, they were in open country. The day before the breakthrough, Ludendorff told the Kaiser that Germany had reached the limit of its resources and that the war must be ended.

The Allied offensive continued, the French and the Americans joining in along their sectors of the front. Back in Germany, largely due to the Royal Navy's relentless blockade, the people were starving. Revolution threatened as anti-war rioters took to the streets and the Imperial High Seas Fleet mutinied. Germany's allies – Austria-Hungary, Turkey and Bulgaria – were on the point of capitulation. On 9 November, the Kaiser was forced to abdicate. He fled to neutral Holland. Two days later, a new republican government in Berlin requested an armistice.

The terms the Allies insisted on were harsh. Matthias Erzberger, the Centre Party politician charged with negotiating with Marshal Foch, failed to secure anything but the most trivial of concessions. Early in the morning of 11 November, as he signed the armistice document, he warned that 'a people of 70 million are suffering, but they are not dead'. Foch pointedly ignored him.

At the eleventh hour of the eleventh day of the eleventh month, the armies ceased fighting along the entire Western Front. Captain Cecil Gray, serving with the Canadian Machine Gun Corps, recorded how his troops took the news. 'Every man had a grin from ear to ear on his face. Nobody yelled or showed uncontained enthusiasm – everybody just grinned – and I think the cause was that the men couldn't find words to express themselves.' As the guns fell silent, birdsong was heard in no man's land, some said for the first time in four years. The Great War – the 'war to end all wars' – was finally over.

VICTORY AT LAST
British troops cheer as an officer reads the news that the armistice has been signed. Sergeant-Major Richard Tobin of the Royal Naval Division recorded how he felt when he heard: 'The Armistice came, the day we had dreamed of. The guns stopped, the fighting stopped. Four years of noise and bangs ended in silence … We were stunned … I should have been happy. I was sad. I thought of the slaughter, the hardships, the waste and the friends I had lost.'

WHAT PRICE VICTORY?

It was peace at last. In the words of Lieutenant Edward Allfree of the Royal Garrison Artillery: 'The war– that long and bloody and ghastly war – was over! Not only over, but it had been won – decisively won – by us and our Allies! The Germans were defeated, crushed! The boastful, bragging Hun, who had started and brought this bloody war on the world, was beaten and in the dust! How entirely comforting! How satisfactory!' Allfree reflected the feelings of most Britons as they celebrated victory.

THE BIG THREE David Lloyd George (left), Georges Clemenceau (centre) and President Woodrow Wilson (right) on their way to the Hall of Mirrors to sign the Treaty of Versailles in June 1919. They had won the war, but were divided as to how best to make the peace.

THE WAR IS OVER

Lloyd George was the hero of the hour. He was cheered to the echo as he led peers and MPs from Parliament across to St Margaret's Church, Westminster, to 'give thanks to Almighty God' for the nation's triumph. In the General Election that December, he and his Coalition partners were swept back to power in a landslide victory. It was the first one in which women were finally allowed to vote, though the franchise was limited to those over 30. They also had to be ratepayers or married to ratepayers.

Peace brought its own problems. Though Britain had been part of a stunning victory, the nation was crippled by the huge debts it had run up to finance the war. The vengeful cried 'Make Germany pay', but whether the Germans were in any position to hand over the vast sums the Allies demanded was a question that no one could answer. And the government had other worries. Bolshevism seemed to be spreading westward from Russia, while in Ireland civil war loomed. At home, Lloyd George's famous promise of 'a land fit for heroes to live in' would come back to haunt him – it was a promise that would prove impossible to fulfil. Britain, it was clear, faced an uncertain future.

Suddenly, it's over

In the end, it was all over dramatically suddenly. Lieutenant Richard Dixon of the Royal Garrison Artillery was on board a leave boat steaming into Folkestone harbour as the armistice came into effect. 'Every craft in there possessing a siren began to let it off', he recalled. 'We on board that leave boat were at first astounded by the noise – what was all the fuss about? But, as it went on and on and we steamed slowly and majestically to our appointed berth and beheld the crews of several ships cheering and waving at us, we tumbled to it. "Dickie", said Captain Brown, "The bloody war's over! It's over!" And it was.'

Meanwhile in London, five minutes before the war officially ended, Lloyd George appeared in Downing Street, setting out for the House of Commons to announce the cessation of hostilities. 'At eleven o'clock', he told the cheering crowd, 'this war will be over. We have won a great victory and we are entitled to a bit of shouting.'

IT'S PEACE AT LAST
A crowd in London celebrates (right) as news of the armistice spread in various ways. Fireworks known as maroons – used during the war as air-raid warnings – were set off now to alert people to the good news. Boy Scouts cycled around the city blowing the 'All Clear' on their bugles, and Big Ben struck the hour for the first time in more than four years. Just as they had on the day that war broke out, huge crowds gathered outside Buckingham Palace, calling for the King and Queen. The royal couple obligingly came out onto the balcony, Queen Mary carrying a small flag, which according to one observer she waved 'violently'. Another recalled how the 'buses had to cease running for the soldiers seized the [sign] boards from the sides and front to help make a big bonfire in Trafalgar Square'. People were celebrating everywhere, some more vengefully than others. In Brackley, Northamptonshire, they hung effigies of the Kaiser and his son, the German Crown Prince, in the street. In Glasgow, Thomas Livingstone 'took Agnes and Tommy [his wife and young son] into town to see the sights'. It was, he recorded in his diary, 'the greatest day in the history of the world'.

'We were told that this was "the war to end war" and some of us at least believed it … All the mud, blood and bestiality only made sense on the assumption that it was the last time civilised man would ever have to suffer it.'

Lieutenant John Nettleton, Rifle Brigade, 1918

Celebrating victory

Shout they did. When Big Ben, which had been silenced since August 1914, tolled out the hour, people erupted in spontaneous celebration. Thousands flocked to Buckingham Palace, chanting 'We want the King!'. George V duly appeared on the balcony with Queen Mary to wave to the vast crowd. Once back inside the palace, he marked the great occasion by breaking open a bottle of vintage brandy, his first alcohol since 1915. It had been laid down by the Prince Regent to celebrate Wellington's victory at Waterloo and tasted, the King noted, 'very musty'.

Across the land, alerted by the sound of the church bells, people poured into the streets. It was one massive party. Everyone was kissing everyone else. In the Ritz Hotel in London, Lady Cynthia Curzon, draped in a vast Union Jack, led the assembled company in singing patriotic songs. Later, according to the young Sir Oswald Moseley, who was later to marry her, she 'tore around Trafalgar Square with the great crowd, setting fire to old cars and trucks'.

Writer and cartoonist Osbert Sitwell later recalled how that night 'it was impossible to drive through Trafalgar Square: because the crowd danced under lights turned up for the first time for four years – danced so thickly that the heads, the faces, were like a field of golden corn moving in a dark wind … They revolved and whirled their partners around with rapture, almost with abandon, yet, too, with solemnity, with a kind of religious fervour, as if it were a duty.'

HOME TO STAY
Soldiers back from France and on their way home to be demobilised queue to change their francs for pounds at a bureau de change in Waterloo Station. Many protested that the whole process of getting them home was taking too long. The *Daily Herald* called on the government to 'send the boys home'. The article continued: 'The war is not officially "over", but everyone knows that in fact it is over. Munition-making has stopped; motorists can joy ride; the King has a drink; society has had its victory ball.' Its trenchant conclusion read: 'Danger of too rapid demobilisation? Bunkum!' Thousands felt the same.

Perched on top of a bus trapped by the crowds between the Royal Exchange and the Mansion House in the City of London, Florence Baker, a VAD at Bethnal Green Military Hospital, was another eyewitness. 'Well, if everywhere else is like London,' she wrote to her mother, 'then all England must be mad!' Indeed, the celebrations were universal. Even in sedate Cheltenham, Lieutenant John Nettleton, who was home from the front on leave, went down to the Promenade and saw 'the people milling about the streets, singing and dancing'.

Mourning the fallen

Not everyone felt like celebrating. Duff Cooper, who was also home on leave, felt 'unable to take part in the enthusiasm. This was the moment to which I had looked forward for four years and, now it had arrived, I was overcome by melancholy. Amid the dancing, the cheering, the waving of flags, I could only think of my friends who were dead.' His mood may have been affected by the fact that he was suffering from the first symptoms of influenza. Around 228,000 were to die in the influenza pandemic that swept the country over the following months. He was one of the lucky ones who lived through the flu as well as the war.

Many others had mixed feelings, too. Victoria Smith, a school girl at the time, recalled how she and her classmates were let out of school as the church bells pealed to signal the armistice. She saw 'the geography mistress, head in hands, quietly but copiously crying. She had been widowed by the war.' The author Vera Brittain – who had lost her fiancé, brother and two close friends to the war – shared the same emotions. Peace, she wrote, 'had come too late for me. All those with whom I had been really intimate were gone: not one remained to share with me the heights and depths of my memories.' In Shropshire, the mother of the war poet Wilfred Owen had particular reason to grieve. An hour after the armistice, a War Office telegram arrived at her home. It told her that her son had been killed a week earlier, mown down by German machine guns as he attempted to lead his men over a rickety bridge across the River Sambre.

FIGHTING SPANISH FLU
A masked cleaner sprays the top of a bus with disinfectant during the great influenza pandemic of 1918-19. 'Spanish flu', as it was termed, killed over 200,000 in Britain and an estimated 50 million worldwide – far more than had been killed on all sides in the entire war. The first wave of the pandemic struck in the summer of 1918, the second that autumn and winter and the third in early 1919. Unlike other pandemics, in which children and the old had been the main victims, this time it was largely young adults who were most at risk. Everyone was terrified of contracting the disease. *The Times* labelled it 'the great plague of influenza'; in Ireland, Molly Deery, a Donegal resident, recalled that 'people were told to keep to one side of the road if someone in a house had it'. The *Dungannon Democrat* reported that 'it can be seen that this is no ordinary influenza but some form of disease which ... baffles the best skill of medical men'.

Bring the boys home!

As for the men at the front, some did not know how to react at first. Many had presumed that they would not live to see the end of the war. Now, the thoughts of most turned to home – they wanted to get out of khaki and back into civilian life as quickly as possible. Demobilisation, though, turned out to be a cumbersome process. It did not start until 9 December and the slowness with which it was carried out – at least initially – fostered active discontent among the now reluctant soldiery. Many wanted to avoid the risk of being posted to Germany, as part of the forces sent to occupy Cologne and the western part of the Rhineland. Still more dreaded the prospect of being despatched to Russia to support the so-called White Russians in their attempt to suppress the revolution.

Trouble started as early as January 1919, when 10,000 soldiers at Folkestone refused to board the ships standing ready to take them back to France. Other protests followed at Dover and Brighton. In Whitehall, soldiers picketed government officers, carrying placards with slogans like 'No more red tape', 'We want civvie suits and 'Promises are not pie crust'. The most serious incident took place at Calais, when thousands of troops rioted, took over their transit camp and refused to return to their units. Haig, certain that the rioters were being 'led astray by Bolshevik agitators', actually proposed that the ringleaders be shot. Government action was needed. Winston Churchill, now Secretary of State for War and Air Minister, came up with a new scheme to speed up the demobilisation process. Soon, according to him, men were being released 'at the enormous rate of 13,000 or 14,000 daily'. By the end of the year, only 125,000 men eligible for release from the army were still waiting.

Putting women back in their place

At home, women were being demobilised as well. Women workers on government contracts received two weeks pay in lieu of notice, a free rail pass and an 'out of work donation'. This was set at 20s a week for the first 13 weeks of unemployment and 15s for the next 13 weeks. After that, it stopped. Some were not sorry to see the women go. The *Leeds Mercury* welcomed the dismissal of the city's female bus conductors. 'Their record of duty well done is seriously blemished by their habitual and aggressive incivility … Their shrewish behaviour will remain one of the unpleasant memories of the war's vicissitudes.' The only areas in which women were really successful in keeping their wartime jobs were in shops and offices. Many were forced back into domestic service.

ADJUSTING TO PEACE

Demobilisation was only one of the many problems confronting Lloyd George and his new government. On paper, his position was impregnable. In continuing partnership with the Unionists, he swept back to power in the December 1918

SIGNING THE TREATY
Allied officers and diplomats stand on chairs and tables in the antechamber to the Hall of Mirrors at Versailles, trying to get a glimpse of the peace treaty being signed on 28 June, 1919. Two days later Lloyd George made a formal announcement to the House of Commons that the treaty had been concluded. He received a standing ovation, but even before he spoke nearly every MP had risen to cheer him and to sing 'God Save the King'. In the debate that followed, the Prime Minister described the terms of the treaty as 'stern but just'. Its aim, he told MPs, was to 'compel Germany, in so far as it is in her power, to restore, to repair and redress'. But even then there were some who doubted the wisdom of the treaty's severity. The writer Harold Nicolson, then a promising young diplomat, wrote that 'the real crime is the reparations and indemnity chapter, which is immoral and senseless'.

STREET PARTY
A children's street party is in full swing on the Isle of Dogs in London's East End. It was held to mark Peace Day – 19 July, 1919 – though the Treaty of Versailles, which officially brought the war to an end, was signed on 28 June. The centrepiece of the occasion was a great military parade through the heart of the capital. Thousands gathered in the streets to cheer. The only moment of quiet came when the troops marched down Whitehall past the temporary Cenotaph that Sir Edwin Lutyens had designed for the occasion. 'The memorial was most impressive', reported the *Sunday Times*, 'with its summit crowned by a great laurel wreath, holding in place a Union Jack that was draped loosely above the monument. On the steps were a number of tiny home-made wreaths and humble garden flowers, placed there by loving hands.' The temporary structure was replaced by a permanent one, officially unveiled on the anniversary of Armistice Day the following year.

'General Jacobs, my corps commander, stood under the Union Jack by a big statue of the Kaiser and took the salute. The men marched with fixed bayonets, wearing their steel helmets and carrying their packs.'

Major Thomas Westmacott, Cologne, 1918

General Election. The Coalition won a staggering 478 seats in the House of Commons – 335 Unionists, 133 Coalition Liberals and 10 Coalition Labour MPs. Non-Coalition Labour held on to 63 seats, but the official Liberals were reduced to a rump of 28 and lost their leader: Asquith was defeated by a Coalition candidate in his East Fife constituency. The rout marked the beginning of the end for the Liberal Party as a significant parliamentary force.

The Irish Nationalist Party was also decimated, winning just seven seats. Sinn Fein, with its demand for immediate, outright Irish independence, captured 73 seats. Out of principal, the Sinn Feiners – including Countess Markowitz, the first women to be elected as an MP – refused to take their seats in Westminster. Early the following year, 29 of them met in Dublin, setting up their own Irish Parliament and proclaiming a republic. A bitter guerrilla war with the British was the inevitable consequence.

'Homes fit for heroes'

The premier looked set for a long term of office – 'Lloyd George can be Prime Minister for life, if he likes', said Andrew Bonar Law, the Unionist leader. But in practice, he soon faced substantial difficulties. The Unionist MPs, on whom the government depended, wanted a speedy return to pre-war normality. This meant the swift dismantling of state controls, letting private enterprise operate freely once more, the reduction of taxes and the abandonment of what they regarded as wasteful welfare schemes. Amid much grumbling, the school leaving age was raised from 12 to 14, but the ambitious housing programme that Lloyd George had promised the electorate – the aim was to build 500,000 new homes in three years – was an early casualty of the drive for economic austerity.

'Make Germany pay!'

Britain had emerged from the conflict as a debtor nation. In order to pay for the war, it had sold 25 per cent of its overseas investments. It had also borrowed prodigiously and now owed more than £1,350 million – over £1,000 million of it to the USA. The question on many people's minds was how would this staggering debt ever be repaid?

The hard-faced Unionists massed on the back benches believed that they had the answer. It was to 'Make Germany pay!'. Sir Eric Geddes, the First Lord of the Admiralty, told the voters: 'We will get everything out of Germany that you can squeeze out of a lemon and a bit more. I will squeeze her until the pips squeak.' Lloyd George, at least at first, seemed inclined to go along with him. At a meeting in Bristol, he declared bluntly that 'we propose to recover the entire cost of the war from Germany'. It was a popular rallying cry, but like another of his pledges – to bring the Kaiser to trial and, if found guilty, to hang him for war crimes – it was one he came to regret.

Luckily for Lloyd George, the plan to try the Kaiser came to nothing when the Dutch refused to give the exiled ex-monarch up for trial. But the pledge to make the Germans pay the bill for the war would not go away. It bedevilled the peacemakers when they came together in Paris, in January 1919, to discuss the terms to be imposed on their defeated enemy. President Wilson, anxious to gain support for his cherished idea of a League of Nations, had sailed from the USA to be among their number. Wilson, Georges Clemenceau (the French premier) and Lloyd George wrangled over many points in the treaty, one of them being the

RETURN FROM THE RHINE
The last British troops prepare to leave their posting at Cologne for home, as the Army of Occupation was slowly withdrawn from western Rhineland. When the British arrived in Cologne, marching over bridges into the city, Major Thomas Westmacott of the 24th Division recorded that he had 'seen a sight today that I shall never forget. There were big crowds of Germans looking on in spite of the rain, but they seemed more curious than anything else. I saw one woman in tears, poor soul, but bar that it might have been almost an English crowd.'

MINISTERING ANGELS
Nurses and soldiers honour war heroine
Edith Cavell as her coffin returns to Dover
in May 1919 (left), shortly to be reburied at
Norwich Cathedral. Cavell had been
arrested by the Germans in Brussels for
helping prisoners to escape. She was tried
by a military tribunal, found guilty and shot
in October 1915. The night before her
execution, she told the chaplain who visited
her in her cell that 'Standing as I do in view
of God and Eternity, I realise that patriotism
is not enough. I must have no hatred or
bitterness for anyone.' She wanted to be
remembered, she said, simply as 'a nurse
who tried to do her duty'. Many thousands
of women volunteered to serve as nurses,
including Vera Brittain (above), who
became a VAD after the deaths of her
brother and fiance at the front. She later
wrote *Testament of Youth*, in which she
condemned the futility of the war but took
some consolation from the opportunities
for emancipation which came to women
as a result.

question of German reparations. Lloyd George now argued for reducing the
amount that Germany would be forced to pay, but the French refused to budge.
The short and long-term consequences would be catastrophic.

After the peace treaty was finally signed at Versailles at the end of June, the
severity of its financial clauses were swiftly denounced by John Maynard Keynes, a
brilliant young Cambridge economist. His *Economic Consequences of the Peace*
became a best-seller. But others attacked the treaty for not being harsh enough.
Marshall Foch, who boycotted the signing ceremony in protest, spoke for the
diehards when he grumbled, 'This is not peace. It is an armistice for 20 years.'

An uncertain future

Despite the pessimists, Britons and their families had no doubts that the country
had won a truly remarkable victory. General Smuts, premier of South Africa and a
member of Lloyd George's War Cabinet, told his fellow colonial leaders that the
empire had 'emerged from the war quite the greatest power in the world, and it is
only unwisdom or unsound policy that could rob her of that great position'.
With the acquisition of the League of Nations mandates over Palestine,
Tanganyika and Iraq as part of the peace settlement, the British Empire had
reached its greatest territorial extent.

ALCOCK AND BROWN – NON-STOP ACROSS THE ATLANTIC

Intrepid aviators John Alcock (on the left) and Arthur Brown (right) were both military pilots during the war, but they achieved lasting fame by becoming the first to fly non-stop across the Atlantic. They made their historic flight in a converted Vickers Vimy IV bomber, powered by twin Rolls-Royce engines, and are seen here enjoying a celebratory breakfast after the event. They took off from Newfoundland early in the afternoon of 14 June, 1919, getting into the air before their rivals, who were still test-flying their Handley-Page aircraft. The flight was cold and arduous; more than once they flew upside down in dense freezing fog, while Brown crawled out onto the wings to chip off ice. After sixteen-and-a-half hours of flying, they reached their destination – Ireland. The landing, in a bog, was less than perfect (below). People on the ground tried to warn them and direct them to a nearby airstrip, but Alcock and Brown just thought they were being greeted and waved cheerfully back. Their rewards were national acclaim, a £10,000 prize put up by the *Daily Mail* and knighthoods from the King.

Certainly, the great victory parade in London that followed the conclusion of the Treaty of Versailles seemed to bear Smuts out. For hour after hour, the crowds watched the participants pass by. They included stalwart blue-jackets from the greatest navy in the world and soldiers from the largest army the British had ever raised. Australians, New Zealanders, Canadians, Indians and representatives from all the other colonies took part. There were the guns that had deluged the enemy with millions of shells and, grinding by on their tracks, tanks, the new war-winning weapon created and pioneered by British inventiveness and engineering genius. Above people's heads, the Royal Air Force staged a fly-past. With more than 20,000 aircraft at its disposal, it, too, was the biggest in the world.

The celebrations would be short-lived. The brief post-war boom soon turned to bust and as the dole queues lengthened thousands of ex-servicemen found themselves without jobs. Many began to question whether it had all been worthwhile. Through the winning of its great victory, had Britain sowed the seeds of its eventual decay and decline?

GRIM REALITY

A demobilised NCO wears his two discharge medals on a threadbare suit (right), while two disabled veterans make paper flowers for the Ypres League at a workshop in London's Old Kent Road (left). Roughly a quarter of the men who returned home from the war were suffering some degree of physical disability; lost limbs were common. The government eventually agreed to pay pensions, but the rates were set on a sliding scale. They were also mean. A fully disabled man got just £1 5s a week, with an extra 2s 6d for each child. It was not until 1921 that the Pensions Act raised disability pensions to a semi-respectable level. Even for the fully fit, jobs were hard to come by, especially after the brief post-war boom fizzled out. George Coppard, who had served as a machine-gunner, remembered bitterly 'Lloyd George and company had been full of talk about making the country fit for heroes to live in, but it was just so much hot air. No practical steps were taken to rehabilitate the broad mass of demobbed men … there were no jobs for the "heroes" who haunted the billiard halls as I did.'

INDEX

PICTURE ACKNOWLEDGEMENTS

Abbreviations: t = top; m = middle; b = bottom; r = right; c = centre; l = left

All images in this book are courtesy of Getty Images, including the following which have additional attributions:
Front cover, 4, 17, 20r, 27b, 37b, 41, 42, 61, 64tl, 64bl, 68, 106, 108, 122b, 129, 130-131, 132b, 136t, 139,
    140-141, 143: Popperfoto
57, 71, 75, 95, 98bl, 112, 116, 125: Time & Life Pictures
67b, 132t: Roger Viollet
80t: Sean Sexton
115t: George Eastman House

LOOKING BACK AT BRITAIN
THE END OF A WORLD – 1910s
is published by The Reader's Digest Association Ltd,
London, in association with Getty Images and
Endeavour London Ltd.

Copyright © 2009 The Reader's Digest Association Ltd

The Reader's Digest Association Ltd
11 Westferry Circus
Canary Wharf
London E14 4HE
www.readersdigest.co.uk

Endeavour London Ltd
21–31 Woodfield Road
London W9 2BA
info@endeavourlondon.com

Written by
Jeremy Harwood

For Endeavour
Publisher: Charles Merullo
Designer: Tea Aganovic
Picture editors: Jennifer Jeffrey, Franziska Payer Crockett
Production: Mary Osborne

For Reader's Digest
Project editor: Christine Noble
Art editor: Conorde Clarke
Indexer: Marie Lorimer
Proofreader: Ron Pankhurst
Pre-press account manager: Dean Russell
Product production manager: Claudette Bramble
Production controller: Sandra Fuller

Reader's Digest General Books
Editorial director: Julian Browne
Art director: Anne-Marie Bulat

Colour origination by Chroma Graphics Ltd, Singapore
Printed and bound in China

We are committed both to the quality of our
products and the service we provide to our customers.
We value your comments, so please do contact us on
08705 113366 or via our website at
www.readersdigest.co.uk

If you have any comments or suggestions about
the content of our books, email us at
gbeditorial@readersdigest.co.uk

ISBN: 978 0 276 44397 8
BOOK CODE: 638-009 UP0000-1
ORACLE CODE: 356900009H.00.24
CONCEPT CODE: UK 0154/L/S